CULTURE

A GUIDE FOR LEADERS

SHOCK

IGNITING AN INTEGRITY AND PURITY REVOLUTION

BY JULIE HIRAMINE
WITH THE GENERATIONS OF VIRTUE TEAM

Julie and the team would like to dedicate
this book to the next generation.

Published by Standard Publishing, Cincinnati, Ohio
www.standardpub.com

Printed in: United States of America
Acquisitions editor: Robert Irvin
Cover design: Scott Ryan
Interior design: Thinkpen Design, Inc., www.thinkpendesign.com

ISBN 978-0-7847-3306-6

16 15 14 13 12 11   1 2 3 4 5 6 7 8 9

CONTENTS

FOREWORD

It was a crisp Friday evening late in my senior season as the star quarterback of state powerhouse Thomas Jefferson High School. I'd been playing the game of my life while our team was vying for a state playoff berth against our brawny, budding rival Bettendorf High. I'd already ripped off two fifty-yard runs for touchdowns earlier in the game, and now as we broke huddle and I crouched under center for the last play, I awaited a snap that would stab one more gridiron foe straight through the heart.

Sure, we were down 26–24. Sure, we were on our own twenty-five-yard line. Still, we had them right where we wanted them. At the snap, my wide receiver, Randy Jacobson, blitzed past the defensive back on a post pattern, my favorite play. The crowd gasped. Randy was one of the fastest guys in the state, and with five yards of separation between him and the defender, everyone knew that there was no one in the stadium who could chase him down. The timing on the play was perfect, and I'd have hit him in perfect stride with a perfect strike—had Randy been 6'2". The trouble was, Randy was only 5'8".

Thrown a mere six inches too high, the tight spiral glanced off his hands and hit the turf. Game over.

That awful moment is frozen in time and etched indelibly into my mind. Had I thrown that ball only six inches lower, Randy would have scored, Jefferson would have won the conference title and earned a spot in the playoffs, and I would have likely made an all-state team. The bigger promotions never materialized, either. While scholarship offers came, no top-tier, Division I coaches offered me a place where I could make a real impact on the national scene.

These were the most glorious—and desperate—dreams of my heart. I'd worked out twice a day the entire off-season to make them a reality. I'd sacrificed so many relationships and so much fun. Now those dreams were gone.

Six inches.

Perhaps you're wondering how the story of an overthrown pass from years ago applies to your youth ministry, or to the many lives around you that you are impacting for God. Not everyone gets to play quarterback, but every last one of you has desperate, yearning dreams about ministry and impacting lives that rest on that same critical distance—six inches. That distance between the *heart* and the *head*.

That short distance is the approximate span between *knowing* God's standards for sexual purity for your group (what's in your head) and *living out* those standards completely in your own relationships and in your teachings (what's in your heart). When it comes to your life in God, that distance couldn't be more important. In my own case, that distance had a far bigger impact on my life and ministry than a mere six inches on an incomplete fourth-quarter pass.

Just as it was one distant Friday night on Bettendorf's field, wins and losses and promotions can all rest on a span as small as the distance between heart and head. The same is true when it comes to wins and losses in your relationships and in your promotions of God's kingdom. **Too often, we ignore that six-inch distance between our heads and hearts, paying far too much attention to what we say about integrity and relationships and far too little attention to our *actions*** regarding the same subjects.

A lack of integrity in our relationships is pervasive today, not only in the lives of our teens but in our personal lives as well, especially in the way we treat each other sexually. So many teens in today's society have learned to push across each other's sexual boundaries. Why does it seem so hard to be who we say we are these days?

Without a doubt, the media was the key culprit in my life, and I suspect many of us, leaders and teens alike, have the same problem. It is the one big thing that keeps us double-minded in our relationships and in our teaching. We see how relationships are done in the movies, on the small screen, in music, in magazines—even on our phones!—and it is too easy to slip into those patterns because that's what we've seen and what we're familiar with. We often don't think; we just copy. It's far easier to merely mimic the world's standards about sex, dating, and relationships instead of teaching boldly and plowing the field to sow the seeds of purity in our own churches.

If we actually understood how much we're being influenced by media, we would probably stop consuming the vast chunks of it that we do, and we would most likely advise our teens to do the same. If we were clear on the massive impact the songs, television shows, and movies we take in are having on the way we live and on the decisions we make, we would surely change. And we would want to, because we wouldn't knowingly turn our minds over to such a controlling and manipulative force.

Trouble is, we don't. Our teens are left believing the same lies we believed at their age, and then some: *It isn't love if you aren't in bed. . . . Real chemistry can't happen without the physical play. . . . Sex is just a physical thing, and it won't hurt either of you. . . . The quickest way to get to know someone is to go all the way. . . . True beauty is truly sensual. . . . The more you date, the more likely you'll find the right one. . . . Pursuing multiple relationships is just good time management.* The lies go on and on, and no one stops to think them all through in any practical way.

Far too often, these myths get rooted in our teens' hearts a lot more easily than the truths of God, and that critical six inches from the head to the heart might as well be six million. What do we do?

We surely need to stop consuming certain media. As I came to understand more of the impact of media on my thinking during my early years with Christ, the Lord led me to dump all my old secular records and to replace them with contemporary Christian music, and to become tighter and tighter on my movie and television standards and in the way I protected my eyes and my mind from the sensuality around me. This led to rapid spiritual growth for me, and similar decisions can make for important steps for many people.

But what about positive, helpful intervention for others, including our teens? We need practical, memorable, purposeful instruction to reverse what the media has done in the hearts of our young people. And we need a means to help them evaluate and use media in healthy ways as they go forward.

That's why I'm so excited about *Culture Shock*. Julie Hiramine and the Generations of Virtue team have put together a five-session game plan to give you the tools you need for victory in your teens' lives. It's not going to be easy, but if you have a passion to help them close the too-prevalent gap between their hearts and minds, then keep reading. Let's teach our young people that having a life full of adventure and an awesome, God-crafted love story aren't impossible things. They're real—and they can be theirs! Take this guide for leaders and dig deep into your own heart first. Allow God to speak to you and get to your heart like never before. May your life, your walk, and your teaching never be the same again.

For God's kingdom,

Fred Stoeker
Coauthor, Every Young Man's Battle
and Every Man's Battle series

DEAR LEADER,

Culture casts its mold on us, squeezing us into its image. Breaking free from that mold is what this book is all about. A distinctly different mold needs to be formed—one that is in the image of Jesus Christ.

God is calling a generation of pure-hearted, valor-seeking world changers who will not bend or bow to the taunting voice of the enemy in our culture today. There is a growing remnant of young people being armed to turn the tide of this country, of this world, back to Christ. This set-apart generation is wholeheartedly pursuing their destiny, determined to fulfill the calling and plan that God has on their lives.

And this generation is in your church, in your small group, on your campus, and in your home.

But these potential world changers are in desperate need of leaders who can stand with them against our culture. There are more challenges today than ever before in regard to sexual purity, due to provocative media and our sex-absorbed culture, among other things. But as you read through *Culture Shock*, take heart! You're not in this alone!

This revolution of purity and integrity is God's message, his idea, and his agenda. The Lord God Almighty is backing up your stand for purity 100 percent, and he will give you every tool you need to equip this generation to stand strong. I pray that *Culture Shock* is one of those very tools.

Julie Hiramine

FOUNDER, GENERATIONS OF VIRTUE

★ START HERE ★

Skim the magazine racks, flip on the TV, or make a few clicks on the Internet and we get smacked in the face with it. Hypersexuality, obscenity, perversion. All aggressively marketed directly at us. Add in the world's definitions of tolerance, acceptance, spirituality, and truth, and the lines between right and wrong start getting pretty fuzzy.

And if it's difficult for us to ride these waves of life, imagine what's it's like for our youth. The teen years are a critical time—kids are working through school, finding friends, navigating relationships with their parents, discovering their passions, and figuring out who they are and what they've been created to do. And every day they face peer pressure, gossip, ever-spreading technology, and media's constant flow into their lives. Our teens have a lot of complicated questions, and they could use someone willing to point them toward the Lord. What are we going to do about it?

Enter *Culture Shock*, a five-session interactive teen event designed to empower our youths to take a stand against the toxic tide we now find ourselves immersed in. Designed by people who have known this struggle and tested by thousands of teens all around the world, the activities, discussions, and connections presented in this resource will walk your teens through God's truth, helping them to discover their purpose in Christ.

Through these sessions teens will find that there is indeed one Way and one Truth, no matter what lies Satan tries to feed us. As you lead your teens through dynamic games, engaging scenarios, and relevant discussions, you'll be bringing them to the realization that the God who made the world and came down to save it is the same God who has an amazing design for romance, relationships, and every aspect of our lives.

Each session is grounded in God's Word and designed specifically to get teens thinking intentionally about their pursuit for purity and to help them develop strategies for keeping their integrity intact. And in every session you will find helpful leader's tips, talking points, discussion questions, supply lists, and ideas for use with large or small groups, weekend retreats, and camps. Also included are suggestions for connecting with parents, and for continuing to move the integrity and purity revolution forward through follow-up messages to your teens.

All you'll need to help you on your way are volunteers committed to honoring God and passionate about teaching and encouraging teens to do the same. Start your event off with lots of energy, and give your students a vision for what they will be talking and thinking about in the coming sessions. All the material in *Culture Shock* is centered around issues that are at the forefront of teens' minds—things they want to talk about and things you need to help them understand. Through these sessions you'll be leading teens to make healthy decisions about such things as sexual temptation, popularity, bullying, relationships, media, and physical, mental, and spiritual purity.

Once you get started, we're positive that you will find *Culture Shock* an effective tool for challenging your kids to stand firm in God's Word and see the world changed by the power of Jesus' name. After all, we've tested it ourselves!

God is calling you to stand up and make his name known to this generation. Don't back down from the truth. It's time to step up and **jump-start your teens to live lives that will radically shock the culture** we live in today and bring glory and honor to the one true God.

THE GENERATIONS OF VIRTUE TEAM

Have questions or want to keep in touch with our team? Head over to www .generationsofvirtue.org for more. You and your teens can also visit our blog at www.apuregeneration.com. We want to hear from you!

CINDERELLA LIED, SUPERMAN DIED

PART ONE

YOU ARE HERE

Welcome to the first Culture Shock session! We've designed this session to help your teens see the lies that they often believe, especially regarding media. Teens consume such an incredible amount of media every day that it—instead of God's Word—has become the main influence for their beliefs on love, sex, and relationships. We're passionate about helping teens see where they have believed the lies of the enemy so that they can break free from those destructive influences. When they've done that, they can walk boldly in the freedom that Christ has to offer.

Before you dive into this session, take some time to:

★ **READ—Read through the session, of course, but also spend time in the Scriptures that are suggested throughout. The main passages to be used are: Matthew 6:24; 26:6-16; Luke 14:11; 1 Corinthians 13; Ephesians 2:10; and Philippians 4:8, 9. Read the surrounding verses or chapters of these passages so you are aware of the context.**

★ **WATCH—In the time leading up to your session or event, watch out for specific examples in television shows, advertising,** movies, video games, magazines, online content, and elsewhere for lies that are aimed at teens. Having these examples fresh in your mind may be helpful as you lead your group.

★ **PRAY—Ask God for wisdom for yourself and your fellow leaders. Pray for humility and patience as you lead discussions with your teens. Pray for specific girls and guys you know who need to hear this message.**

BREAKING IT DOWN

For camps and weekend retreats, it's possible to complete this session in one day. For large groups and small groups, "Cinderella Lied, Superman Died" is an extensive session that could fill several weeks of meetings instead of just one. Here are some breakdown options for your large or small group:

1. Use this as a longer event by breaking it into three sessions:

 * **Session One: Two Truths and a Lie activity and two movie clips with discussion questions**

 * **Session Three: Wrapped in Lies and Throw Away the Lies**

 * **Session Two: Four movie clips with discussion questions**

2. Break it into two sessions:

 * **Session One: Two Truths and a Lie and three movie clips, with discussion questions**

 * **Session Two: Three movie clips with discussion questions, Wrapped in Lies, and Throw Away the Lies**

3. Use this as a one-session event by adjusting the movie clips and discussion questions to fit your time.

THE MAIN EVENT

Once you've decided how to organize your sessions, prepared yourself and your team, gathered your teens, and given it all over to God, you're ready to help ignite an integrity and purity revolution!

SEND THIS MESSAGE

Make this loud and clear to your students from the start:

 * **This generation has a calling and destiny that is amazing! You are a piece in the puzzle and fill a spot no one else can fill.**

LEADER TIP

If your group isn't very interactive, or if your students are just getting to know each other, have team leaders sit with microphones (if needed) in different spots in the audience. The leaders can go through the activities from their seats as opposed to the stage, providing a more comfortable, approachable environment.

★ **How are you going to reach your God-given destiny? How are you going to change the world? You have to start where it counts:**

Identify and overcome lies you believe that hold you back from fulfilling your calling in Christ.

OPEN UP

Here's a suggestion for opening the session with prayer:

Heavenly Father, we thank you so much for this opportunity to learn from you and help one another. We ask that you would meet us here and cause us to grow and change to become more like your Son. Jesus, we ask that your presence would stop any distractions that might keep anyone here from coming closer to you. We thank you for all that you are going to accomplish with this event. In Jesus' name, amen.

ACTIVITY: TWO TRUTHS AND A LIE

Have each of your leaders share three brief statements—facts or events—from his or her life. All three should be things that others might find to be unbelievable about that person. Two of these points will be true and one will be false.

Let your students have the opportunity to vote for the point they think is false. Make sure to say all three of the points first and then repeat them before the teens vote. Then as each point is said again, the students can stand up after they hear the point they believe to be false. Allow time for each leader to reveal his or her truths, and if there is a cool story behind the true statements, take a moment to tell it!

Goal: To show how easy it is to tell and believe lies, whether those lies come through relationships or the media.

> **LEADER TIP**
> A great option if you can prep some of your more mature students beforehand: allow students to do this as well. Let one or two share their three points after the leaders. Keep the pace moving, but it's always fun to engage students with one another.

Here are some (real-life) examples of Two Truths and a Lie:

Tim

1. I love to sword fight. (Truth)
2. I was born premature, and without a butt. (Truth)
3. I was in the army for four years. (Lie)

Isaac

1. I'm part Indian. (Truth)
2. I LOVE singing country music in the shower as loud as I can. (Lie)
3. I once kissed a cat. (Truth)

LEADER TIP

Be sure your leaders switch up the order in which they place their truths and lies so it's more difficult for the teens to guess. For instance, one leader should order the statements as truth, lie, truth. Another, lie, truth, truth.

FOR SMALL GROUPS

All your group members can think of two things that are true about themselves and one that is a lie. One by one, let each student share with the group, and see if the others can guess the lies.

FOR WEEKEND RETREATS

If there's time, have the students get into small groups and try this activity out on each other! Be sure to mix up the usual groups of teens. They tend to travel in packs (as any youth leader knows!), so make it a goal to get them to hang out with other people in the youth group.

FOR CAMPS

Before your students arrive for a main session, let them do Two Truths and a Lie in their cabins with their camp counselors. It's a great settling-in game or an over-the-dinner-table game. Either way, it's a fantastic icebreaker.

Then, in a main session, allow time for all the camp counselors who will be speaking that week to stand up and go through this activity. The students will be familiar with it from having done it in their cabins or at their first meal.

LIES WE BELIEVE

To introduce the next section, a team member can describe a lie he or she believed. This can be a serious lie, such as, "I believed there were no consequences for my sexual actions," or take a more lighthearted approach. After the person talks about the lie, he or she can share some of the Key Points About Lies (see list below) and, if time allows, ask the group for suggestions of other common lies people believe.

Goal: To make the teens you work with feel more comfortable with revealing their experiences and also to start helping them identify the more common lies that they believe. They may be lies like "If I just had what I wanted, I'd be happy" or "If I'm not sleeping with someone, then I'm not loved or accepted." See a whole list of Sample Lies on page 18.

The following is an example from our team:

> **From Kelsey:** I had a slight problem in high school—I believed the lie that I deserved to be worshipped. You know how it is, always trying to look perfect, to be the best. One day I decided that my sister's jeans would be the perfect way to get attention. Now keep in mind, my sister is about three sizes smaller than me. Well, I somehow managed to squeeze into the jeans and kept it together all day . . . until choir practice. When our director instructed all the students to sit down on the bleachers, my pants split from waist to ankle! Thank God it was an all-girls' choir! After the embarrassment wore off, the Lord used that example to show me how I had wrongly pursued worship and attention for myself, instead of directing it where it rightly belongs, on Christ.

KEY POINTS ABOUT LIES

While most of us were taught not to tell lies, many of us were never taught not to *believe* lies.

★ **The enemy thrives on lies because getting you to believe lies will keep you from your calling.**

★ **In John 8:44, Jesus said to the Jews who were looking to kill him: "You belong to your father, the devil, and you want to carry out your father's desires. He was a murderer from the beginning, not holding to the truth, for there is no truth in him. When he lies, he speaks his native language, for he is a liar and the father of lies."**

★ **Lies have a way of building on each other, creating something like a pyramid. These pyramids can get so big that we can't see the truth anymore. Lies can be blinding, but the blindness may happen slowly, over a long time.**

★ **In Isaiah 28, the people in power did not want to listen to God. They boasted (v. 15): "We have entered into a covenant with death. . . . We have made a lie our refuge and falsehood our hiding place." The last place we want to be is in a refuge of lies.**

★ **The only way to see the truth, versus a lie, is through the Word of God, because God's Word is absolute truth. "Everything that was written in the past was written to teach us, so that through the endurance taught in the Scriptures and the encouragement they provide we might have hope" (Romans 15:4).**

YOUR VIEW

Write down your own notes here about points you want to remember for your group's event.

SAMPLE LIES TO TALK ABOUT

- It's too hard to serve God.
- I can't fulfill my calling.
- Celebrities have the best lives—and I'm stuck here.
- It is no big deal if I sleep with my girl-friend.
- It's totally OK to be gay.
- My parents don't love me.
- "Friends with benefits" is what every-body is doing—it's OK as long as both people agree.
- If I was drunk when it happened, it doesn't count.
- Oral sex isn't really sex.
- We love each other, so sex is totally all right.
- I'd be sooo happy if I was just with _____ (insert latest/greatest celebrity, or the most popular guy/girl in school).
- It doesn't matter what I do now; I can always ask for forgiveness later.
- It doesn't matter what I do as long as no one gets hurt.
- Nobody would miss me if I was gone.

YOUR VIEW

Write down examples of lies the enemy wants your teens to believe.

★ **Have you ever felt like you just didn't know what was true and what was not? It is critical to guard our minds against the lies of the enemy. How do you do that? Philippians 4:6-8 might give you a clue:**

Do not be anxious about anything, but in every situation, by prayer and petition, with thanksgiving, present your requests to God. And the peace of God, which transcends all understanding, will guard your hearts and your minds in Christ Jesus. Finally, brothers and sisters, whatever is true, whatever is noble, whatever is right, whatever is pure, whatever is lovely, whatever is admirable—if anything is excellent or praise-worthy—think about such things.

★ **Romans 1:21-25 (check it out below) talks about exchanging the truth of God for a lie. In what ways have you seen people do that very thing?**

For although they knew God, they neither glorified him as God nor gave thanks to him, but their thinking became futile and their foolish hearts were darkened. Although they claimed to be wise, they became fools and exchanged the glory of the immortal God for images made to look like a mortal human being and birds and animals and reptiles. Therefore God gave them over in the sinful desires of their hearts to sexual impurity for the degrading of their bodies with one another. They exchanged the truth about God for a lie, and worshiped and served created things rather than the Creator— who is forever praised.

★ **Do you know how you are being lied to? Worldly wisdom would have you believe that a counterfeit version of the truth is far greater than what God designed for you. Remember the deceptive words of the serpent? "You won't die. God knows that the moment you eat from that tree, you'll see what's really going on. You'll be just like God" (Genesis 3:4, 5, *The Message*). Take time this week to seek God's wisdom about how you are being lied to—even in the little ways.**

★ **Check out "Sword Fighting" in part one of *Culture Shock: A Survival Guide for Teens* for more ideas on using Scripture to fight lies.**

AT THE MOVIES

We've always considered movie clips an integral part of this Culture Shock session. The fun part is that you can pick and choose which clips best fit your needs and ages. Let's say you're

LEADER TIP
If you have the option, break out the popcorn during the movie clips! Snacks are almost always a good idea.

really wanting to address dating and relationships; you can choose movie clips that expose lies of the enemy about love and romance. Maybe materialism is a big problem with your teens; you can choose clips that will help your kids see that money isn't everything. Your options are endless! Mix the clips up to keep things fun and fresh with your students.

For this session, jump on a website that will enable you to legally download relatively inexpensive, legitimate film clips. (We've always found WingClips— www.wingclips.com—to be a great service.) Caution: Use discretion when choosing movie clips, because although a single clip can be appropriate, sometimes an entire movie is not, and you don't want to give your teens the impression that a whole movie is OK for them to watch just because their leader showed a clip from it.

This session works best if a leader emcees the movie clips. One effective method is to make it something like a movie review show, where two team members bounce key points off each other (star rating system not required, though it could be fun!). The team members relate the Key Discussion Points after each clip.

Or simply show the clip and then lead a freewheeling discussion with your teens about the scene, exposing the lies contained within it.

After each suggested movie clip we've included here, there are discussion questions that can be used whether you're in large groups, small groups, or at a weekend retreat or a camp session (for whole groups). We've also added questions specifically for guys-only and girls-only groups. If you want to break into guy and girl groups, explain to the whole group beforehand how that will happen, who will go where, and so forth.

The clips that follow, of course, are only suggestions. You can choose your own movie clips, key points, and discussion questions. Go for it—be creative!

GOALS

Before starting, challenge your students to:

1. Discern the objective of the makers and producers of the film. Every producer, director, actor, and scriptwriter has an objective. There's a message they're trying to convey through their movie, and that message isn't always good.

LEADER TIP

Teens love it when you get into it. If you have the ability, convert your meeting room, sanctuary, living room, cabin—or wherever—into a movie-themed area. Get movie posters and pass out tickets for the event. Use stadium seating to make it feel like a real movie theater. Are your kids planning a summer mission trip? Use this opportunity to sell popcorn, candy, and drinks as a fundraiser.

2. Ask themselves, whenever they consume any kind of media: What message is coming through? Is it *helpful* to me, in my relationship with God and with others? Is it pushing me forward or pulling me back?

MOVIE CLIP: *Robots* (2005). Play the scene where the new boss is discussing the new slogan for the company. **THE MESSAGE:** "Why be you when you can be new?"

KEY DISCUSSION POINTS

★ **One message that comes across through this clip is "You aren't good enough the way you are."**

★ **Many people say, "It's all about the money! Advertisers, moviemakers, and so forth only want you to buy what they are selling." Sometimes it can be hard to tell what is true and what is just for sale.**

★ **Some people or companies will influence your thoughts about yourself any way they can in order to get you to buy their product.**

★ **The enemy will always lie to you and say, "You'll be happy when you have this, that, and the other thing." But true contentment is only found in Christ.**

DISCUSSION QUESTIONS FOR ALL

1. The lie in this clip is pretty obvious: you're not good enough the way you are. What are some ways you've seen this message in your own life? What is true or false about it?

2. What ways do you go about finding out the truth? How do you tell if you're being told a lie?

3. If you're listening to *anyone* else's view of you besides God's, you will always end up being confused about who you really are. We need to get into the Word of God and find out what our true identity is. The Bible says, "For you died, and your life is now hidden with Christ in God" (Colossians 3:3). That's an incredibly powerful statement! So if our lives are hidden, how do we find our identity?

BEHIND THE SCENES: HAVE YOUR STUDENTS LOOK UP, READ, AND DISCUSS MATTHEW 6:24 AND EPHESIANS 2:10.

DISCUSSION QUESTIONS FOR GIRLS

(Make sure a female leader takes your girls through this discussion.)

1. How much does media affect your self-image? From your body shape to your complexion to the car you drive, the phone you have, and the clothes you wear, media has an input on all these things. How do you deal with the pressure culture puts on you to be "perfect" or to be someone other than who you are?

2. The objective of marketing isn't to make you want the product being sold. The objective is to make you feel like you *need* what's being sold. Advertisers don't come to you and simply say, "Hey, look at this really cool *new* product we have!" They often say, "Look at this cool, new product we have. If you still have the old one, that is *so* totally stupid. You need an upgrade. You need the best." If you were honest with yourself, would you say that this kind of marketing message works on you? When are you most tempted to have the newest, latest, and greatest?

3. Did you know that if you fulfill the world's expectations of you, you won't fulfill God's plan for your life? You can't be both the world's ideal and God's girl. A lot of times during our teen years, we feel like we can have the best of both worlds. We can be a great Christian at church and party every other night of the week. Does church help us grow and change and learn? Absolutely! But only if we are going with a truly repentant heart, an open mind to the Lord, and a deep desire to change. Otherwise, we will continually fall back into the same patterns of sin. How can you keep focused on God's plan for you? What do you think might happen if you lived out your faith in every area of your life?

4. Read this story from our team:

I could have posed as the poster child for *Good Christian Girl* magazine (if there ever was such a thing). Well, maybe not every night of the week, but certainly at youth group, Bible study, and church! I truly believed that as long as I maintained my "Christian" schedule, what I did the rest of the time didn't really count. I figured that my good works would outweigh my mistakes and I would come out on top in the end. I desperately wanted to be just like the girls I saw on MTV, but just go for a little more Spirit and a little less cleavage around the Christian crowd. I allowed media to shape who I was, totally and completely. If I saw some superstar wearing an outfit in *People* magazine, I'd go get it. If I knew there was a new celebrity diet on the market, I'd try it too. It wasn't until I gave up watching and reading and listening to all the secular media that I had allowed to influence me that I was truly able to change. I had to let go of the world's version of me in order to gain God's perspective on my life and why I was created.

22 ☆ CULTURE SHOCK

Can you relate to that story? Why or why not? How have you allowed media to shape who you are, what you do, and what you view as valuable? What do you feel convicted to change?

 BEHIND THE SCENES: DISCUSS MATTHEW 6:24.

DISCUSSION QUESTIONS FOR GUYS

(Make sure a male leader takes your guys through this discussion.)

1. From your body shape to your complexion to the car you drive, the phone you have, and the clothes you wear, media has an input on all these things. How do you deal with the pressure culture puts on you to be "perfect" or to be someone other than who you are? How much is your self-worth tied into how well you perform? What's wrong with that picture?

2. Marketers are smart. They don't just tell you about a product, they make you feel like you *need* that product to get what you want. And what do you want? Well, they'll tell you that too. Media messages shape what you think of as the "good life" and show you the way to get there. They may even try to convince you that the way to Heaven can be earned—through being the best athlete, or having the coolest stuff and the hottest girl-friend. They tell you that you *can* get satisfaction. But what do you think? Where can you find fulfillment?

3. Advertising can be really distracting. Trying to get the newest, latest, and greatest thing can be a never-ending quest. Be honest with yourself—how many times a day do you think you get distracted by media messages? What are three things you could do every day to keep your focus on God's plan for you?

4. Read this story from our team:

> I spent years masking who I was from the church crowd. On Sunday mornings, I'd roll out of bed—hungover from the night before—show up at church to play in the worship band, and then leave early to have a Saturday-night repeat. It was a vicious cycle that kept me bound for most of my teen years. I never really thought anything of it, because everything I watched and listened to told me that my actions were totally fine. Over time, I began to believe what the shows said to me and what the songs sang to me was . . . truth. However, even when I had everything I thought I wanted, I still wasn't happy. Something huge was missing in my life. I began realizing that although my mind kind of wanted God, my body wanted nothing to do with him. That

strain and stress, having the knowledge of truth but no follow-through, began eating me up inside. It wasn't until I was willing to acknowledge God as my Lord and Savior—not just over who I pretended to be, but who I really was—that things really changed in my life. I came to such a broken stage that I willingly gave up all the trashy shows, songs, life patterns, and movies to pursue an incredible relationship with my Lord. It was one of the best decisions I ever made.

Can you relate to that story? Why or why not? How have you allowed media to shape who you are, what you do, and what you view as valuable? What do you feel convicted to change?

 BEHIND THE SCENES: DISCUSS PHILIPPIANS 4:8, 9.

 MOVIE CLIP: *A Cinderella Story* (2004). Play the batting practice scene.
THE MESSAGE: Virtual relationships are just as good as face-to-face ones.

KEY DISCUSSION POINTS

★ **Lie: Virtual relationships are good enough. Talking and interacting with someone face-to-face is overrated.**

★ **Lie: You can really "know" someone as a person in the virtual world.**

★ **Lie: Love is a one-shot deal. If you don't jump on the first relationship that comes along, you will miss out on love for the rest of your life. It's now or never.**

DISCUSSION QUESTIONS FOR ALL

1. Have you ever known someone who was one way face-to-face and completely different online or through texting? Can you see how you can use the Internet to become anyone you want to be versus who you actually are? When you're online, do your profile and conversations reflect who you *really* are? In what ways are you pretending to be someone you're not?

2. Let's take a minute to talk about your text messages. Do they honor God? your parents? your pastor? If you were face-to-face with the person you were texting, would you still say the same things? How would your messages change if you knew they were all going to be posted on a big screen at church? Give examples.

3. There is an overwhelming lie in our culture that says, "You only have one shot at love!" But if you are following God's commands and pursuing his purposes for your life, do you

think he will just let your love life go under the radar and not care about what happens to your relationships? God cares about *every* detail of our lives, especially the people we choose to give our hearts to. The person God has designed for you is crafted to fit you perfectly. If you are pursuing the life Jesus wants for you, he will bless your future love life exceedingly, abundantly—beyond what you could ever imagine! When you're tempted to start writing your own love story, take a minute and just *slow down*! The person sitting next to you is probably NOT your future spouse. Pop a chill pill and wait for God's timing! Are you willing to take a leap of faith and turn your love story over to God? What does that mean for you?

BEHIND THE SCENES: LOOK UP 1 CORINTHIANS 13. DISCUSS THE IDEA OF LOVE BEING PATIENT. OFTEN WE FEEL THE PRESSURE OF THE MEDIA MESSAGE "I HAVE TO HAVE THIS NOW!" IT'S TOUGH TO COUNTERACT THAT MESSAGE IN OUR OWN LIVES. IT IS CRITICAL TO UNDERSTAND THAT REAL LOVE IS WILLING TO WAIT FOR GOD'S PERFECT TIMING.

DISCUSSION QUESTIONS for GIRLS

1. Have you ever noticed how easy it is to pour your heart out to a guy through technology (texting, instant messaging, online social networks)? Have you ever said or sent anything from your phone that you now regret? Talk about that time.

2. Have your private messages ever been shown to people you never intended to see them? How did you respond? If it happened in the future, what would you do?

3. Consider this: What if your pastor was looking over your shoulder at every message you sent? Guess what—he is. His name is Jesus. Will this revelation change what you say through texts and online posts? Can you honestly say that your messages and posts honor God? What needs to change?

4. If you know how you shape your own image through text and online sites, what does this tell you about how much to trust the messages and images of others? What's the best way to tell fact from fiction in what people say or do?

BEHIND THE SCENES: MEMORIZE 1 PETER 4:5.

DISCUSSION QUESTIONS for GUYS

1. So by now you know that guys and girls are really different. But guys, listen up: did you know that when you're texting that girl out of pure boredom, or even to ask nicely how her

exam went, she may take that totally differently? Here's a clue: girls overthink everything! Even though you totally don't mean it "like that," she'll take it "like that." In later sessions, we will talk more about how you can avoid leading a girl on, but for now, remember this: be careful who you are talking to and how often and what you are saying. She may take it totally differently from how you intended it. Has that ever happened to you? Have you ever led on a girl unintentionally? Talk about that time.

2. How do you make your intentions clear when casually chatting (in any form) with a girl? In the future, try this: if you're just friends, act like it. Make it clear. You're not being rude by saying, "Hey, just to make sure we're on the same page, I just want to be friends." Girls need to have clear boundaries from you so that there is no confusion. What are your boundaries in this area? Are you clear with them?

3. Do your messages and posts honor God? How would you feel if your sister or mom saw the way you talk to or about girls? When you interact with girls, are you out to be their friend, or are you just after their bodies?

4. If you know how you shape your own image through text and online sites, what does this tell you about how much to trust the messages and images of others? What's the best way to tell fact from fiction in what people say or do?

BEHIND THE SCENES: MEMORIZE 1 TIMOTHY 6:11.

MOVIE CLIP: *The Chronicles of Narnia: The Lion, the Witch and the Wardrobe* (2005). Play the Turkish Delight scene with Edmund and the White Witch on her carriage. THE MESSAGE: The enemy will often tempt us by giving us a little bit of what we want (in Edmund's case, it was power and control) in order to enslave us to him forever. This happens with every kind of sin. Anything from power to worship to lust to greed—Satan has a way of giving us what we think we want, and then before we know it, we're held captive by him.

KEY DISCUSSION POINTS

★ **For a time, Edmund believed that life was all about him and his desires. His drive was simple: glorify self, me, my, mine—who cares what anyone else needs or wants?**

★ **We have to realize that if we allow selfishness to rule in our lives, it will drive us to turn our backs on everything we know and love just to get what we think we want.**

* The enemy will almost always make it a point to give you just a little taste of what you want, just to get you hungry for more, to drive you to sin. This clip is a fantastic example of this. When the White Witch sees Edmund, she finds out his desire, gives him a sampling of his favorite treat, and then promises him she has rooms full of it in her palace. She feeds his lust for more.

* Another great example of a selfish life is that of the disciple Judas Iscariot. Judas managed the finances for Team Jesus. Everything seemed fine until later in the story when we learn that Judas was actually stealing from the treasury (so he was stealing from Christ himself). The Pharisees (the religious leaders in Jesus' time) wanted to get rid of Jesus and convinced Judas to betray him for thirty pieces of silver. Different sources translate that amount of money into different things, but one thing is certain—such an amount could not have been worth a human life, and definitely not worth the life of our Lord. Imagine coming to a place of such envy and selfishness that you would willingly betray the Savior of the world. It is an incredible and terrifying thought. What is even more concerning is the realization that if we allow the same motivations into our lives, we too could do outrageous and horrible things in order to get what we think we want.

DISCUSSION QUESTIONS FOR ALL

1. You might look at Edmund and say "I'd never do that!" But do you gossip and backbite against one another? Do you aim to make yourself number one and put other people down? That may not be as extreme as what Edmund did, but it is betrayal all the same. Has your greed ever driven you to trample on someone else's feelings?

2. Guarding our hearts against selfishness can be a really tough thing to do. We will talk more about this concept during "Escaping Normal." But for now, can you identify any area where you have been self-seeking instead of Christ-seeking? Talk about that.

3. How can these areas be changed in your life? What are some easy things you can do to change your selfish desires into Christ-driven desires?

 BEHIND THE SCENES: LOOK UP MATTHEW 26:6-16. CONTRAST THE TWO STORIES IN THIS PASSAGE AND DISCUSS.

DISCUSSION QUESTIONS FOR GIRLS

1. For a few painful moments, think of yourself as Edmund. Actually, most of us have a lot more in common with him than we'd like to admit. Can you think of any similarities?

2. Can you see how Edmund had believed the lie that he was the special one and that he ought to be higher than those around him? Have you ever felt a similar desire to be thought of above others? What did that desire lead you to do?

3. Edmund's seemingly innocent desire for a tasty treat led him to desire even grander things, more than he needed or deserved to have. Has your indulgence in a small desire ever led you to want more? Talk about that time. How can knowing where your weaknesses are be a strength?

BEHIND THE SCENES: LOOK UP MATTHEW 25:40 AND DISCUSS WHO IS IMPORTANT IN GOD'S EYES.

DISCUSSION QUESTIONS FOR GUYS

LEADER TIP
Look up the definition of *meekness* and share it with your guys.

1. Do you operate with a competition mentality? Did you know that always having to come out on top, being the best above all others, gives you the same motives that Edmund had? Edmund wanted to be number one, even within his family. His drive to be the best led him to betray his entire family. How do you think the drive to compete affects the way you treat those around you?

2. Think about times when you have felt the need to be superior or treated like someone special. Why do you think you felt that way? What does the Bible say about who is the greatest? Check out Matthew 18:4.

3. Has a small temptation ever led you to want something more? How can focusing on what's bad in your life or feeling sorry for yourself actually make you more likely to give in to your desires? Instead of feeling like we deserve special treatment, what feelings or thoughts can we focus on to combat temptation?

4. We at GOV have found that it's the little things that encourage humility in life. Let's consider this: Next time a buddy is behind you in line, let him go first. Someone insults you? Let it go, don't try to fight back. Didn't win in that basketball game? Go congratulate the winner. These things will encourage humility in your life and cultivate an attitude of meekness. There isn't anything in the Bible about Jesus always having to win or defend himself or seek his own will. Jesus' life was all about honoring God the Father in every area, and he seriously wasn't after bringing glory or fame or honor to his name. When you honestly look at your life, what do you see? Of course, none of us is perfect, but are you aiming, each and every day, to bring glory to yourself—or to God?

BEHIND THE SCENES: LOOK UP LUKE 14:11. HAVE AN HONEST DISCUSSION ABOUT HOW THIS PASSAGE RELATES TO OUR LIVES.

ACTIVITY: WRAPPED IN LIES

SUPPLIES NEEDED

★ **Scissors**

★ **Three spools of ribbon (or yarn), enough to wrap around a person several times**

★ **A card with Sample Lies (see list below) so you can keep the activity moving and not delay it as you come up with new lies that don't repeat ones already used**

The next illustration is one of the most impactful that we share. We believe that if teens can see how lies keep them tied up and cut off from reality, they're much more likely to move in a direction that will set them free.

> ### LEADER TIP
> Who you use for Wrapped in Lies is important. Be sure to pick an adult leader for this activity. You don't want to choose someone who is struggling with their faith (this could be damaging) or someone who would set a poor example for your group.

You'll need at least three adult leaders and one volunteer to participate in this activity. The team members will be the "wrappers" and the volunteer will be the "wrappee." Three team members proceed by circling the wrappee with their ribbon. Before doing the first circling, they speak a lie about the wrappee's life. The wrappee signifies the acceptance of the lies by grasping hold of the ribbon. (See Sample Lies list below.)

Goal: To demonstrate how Satan gets a foothold in a person's life and how the power of lies can stop us from being the people God created us to be.

Begin with this suggested scenario (or feel free to make up your own!): "Here we have Scott. He's fourteen years old and sits behind you in math class. Although he's a nice kid, he's been believing a lot of lies lately . . ."

Leaders now tell him lies, taken from your list. "Scott" signifies that he believes each lie by accepting the ribbon and holding onto it. (Remember: the ribbon represents the lies.) Begin speaking more sample lies over Scott, and as each lie is spoken, wrap Scott once fully around with the ribbon.

SAMPLE LIES

- I have to be tough to fit in.
- My parents don't really love me.
- God doesn't really care about me.
- In fact, God's holding me back from all the good things.
- I have to be a snob to fit in.

- Sexy girls/hot guys are worth more than the "normal looking" people.
- My parents love my brother or sister more.
- I don't have a purpose.
- God doesn't love me.
- I can do whatever I want.
- I've done things so bad, God could never forgive me.
- My choices don't have consequences.
- Watching porn doesn't affect me.
- Nobody is a virgin anymore! That idea is so stupid.
- I can have sex with my girlfriend—we love each other!

LEADER TIP

This session can address specific issues with your group. You know your students best; hit the tough issues hard during this exercise.

- If I was drunk when I had sex, it doesn't count.
- My teen years are supposed to be for fun! I can catch up with God later. I mean, there is always forgiveness, right?
- Cutting myself hurts only me; it doesn't affect anyone around me.
- I deserve to have this done to me; I'm no better than this.
- I have to do this to survive.

YOUR VIEW

Add more lies to the list, perhaps ones that have been revealed as you've gone through this session.

As you continue with the activity, team members can explain how lies work to keep us wrapped up:

★ It starts with one little lie—no big deal.

★ But soon it's tons of lies— one after another—and Scott is stuck.

★ Now the team leader shouts to Scott: "Run after God!" But . . . Scott can't move at all. He's completely tied up.

★ The team leader says: "God wants you to be a worship leader. So raise your hands to God!" Scott can't; he's totally and completely stuck.

★ The team leader says: "God is calling you—answer your phone!" Since Scott's hands are tied up, he won't be able to move. (For fun, if you can arrange it, actually call Scott's phone, which will be in his pocket.)

★ The team leader announces: "Scott can't do anything. He's tied up in lies."

Team members can then go on to explain Scott's despair: "Scott feels like he has wandered so far from the truth, he isn't sure what to believe. One night after a huge party, Scott feels he has nowhere else to turn. Not knowing what else to do, he reaches for the Bible his parents gave him on his twelfth birthday. He opens his Bible to Hebrews 4:12: 'For the word of God is alive and active. Sharper than any double-edged sword, it penetrates even to dividing soul and spirit, joints and marrow; it judges the thoughts and attitudes of the heart.' Scott knows in his heart that God and his Son, Jesus, are able to set him free from the dangerous mind-sets he has chosen. Scott keeps reading his Bible, and over time, this is what he finds . . ."

At this point, team members pull out scissors. Our team likes to emphasize Hebrews 4:12 as they do this part. It's worth reading through the Scripture again! Sure, we might be using scissors instead of swords, but you get the idea!

As each truth is stated (see Sample Truths), one cord of the ribbon is cut.

SAMPLE TRUTHS

- I am called and created by God (Genesis 1:27).
- I have a purpose and destiny in Christ (Jeremiah 29:11).
- I am a child of God (1 John 5:19).
- There is no condemnation in Christ Jesus (Romans 8:1).
- I am forgiven and free (Matthew 26:28).
- My purity is valuable (Matthew 5:8).
- I am a new creation (2 Corinthians 5:17).
- I am a temple of the Holy Spirit (1 Corinthians 6:19).
- I am accepted by God (Isaiah 41:9).
- God completely understands what I'm going through (Hebrews 4:15).
- God loves me as much as he does everyone else (Romans 2:11).
- I *don't* have to look like the celebrities I see on TV (1 Peter 3:3, 4).
- No matter what happens to me, God will never abandon me (Psalm 27:10; Isaiah 49:15).
- I am made wise by the Lord (Proverbs 2:6).
- I am being made complete (Romans 12:2).
- I am never alone (Deuteronomy 31:6).
- I am strong in Christ (Philippians 4:13).

Before long, Scott is free! Your team leaders can encourage him by saying, "OK, Scott! Now run after God!" Explain that true freedom comes in Christ and in the power of his blood! He is able to free us from anything—from lying to having a bad self-image to lust to anger. Jesus said, "If the Son sets you free, you will be free indeed!" (John 8:36). Here are a couple more Scriptures about freedom you can give to your group:

* "The Spirit of the Lord is on me, because he has anointed me to proclaim good news to the poor. He has sent me to proclaim freedom for the prisoners and recovery of sight for the blind, to set the oppressed free, to proclaim the year of the Lord's favor" (Luke 4:18, 19).

* "Now the Lord is the Spirit, and where the Spirit of the Lord is, there is freedom" (2 Corinthians 3:17).

Allow students to share from the audience following this activity. This is a great time to teach, but also to listen. You may have students who want to talk openly about feeling trapped in lies, or wish to talk one-on-one or in small groups. Before you move on to the next exercise, make sure to emphasize the Key Points About the Truth.

KEY POINTS ABOUT THE TRUTH

* Your calling is incredibly important, and it's a job that only you can do! You are amazingly valuable to the kingdom of God. Regardless of your life situation, YOU ARE HERE for a purpose. It doesn't matter how you were brought into this world. Whether you feel like your parents wanted you or not, *only God* has the ability to give and take away life. If you are here, it is *for a reason*.

* If you want to be set free, you're going to have to begin replacing these disgusting lies with the amazing truth of God's Word. That means you will have to begin reading your Bible regularly—*daily!* Nothing else is able to defeat lies like the absolute truth of God's Word.

* The enemy knows this—so he is always out to make the Bible seem boring and irrelevant. Satan knows the amazing power that the Bible holds. The Word of God holds the ability to radically and permanently change your life forever.

* The Bible says that God himself inspires all Scripture—and God is definitely not boring! He is the all-consuming, all-knowing, all-loving creator of the universe. Every sight you see and even things you can't see, he has created! That is not boring!

* Find out more of the truth about you in the "Which Guy/Girl Are You?" quizzes in *Culture Shock: A Survival Guide for Teens.*

ACTIVITY: THROW AWAY THE LIES

When you close "Cinderella Lied, Superman Died," ask the teens to take a few minutes to identify some of the lies they've believed. Ask your leaders to pass out note cards and have the teens write down three lies they now recognize that they have been accepting as truth. It's a good idea to ask team members to share some sample lies while the teens are writing. This sort of vulnerability from their leaders will help your students think more deeply about and identify the lies in their lives.

Often, this activity is surprisingly powerful, as many teens have never realized how much garbage they've believed throughout their lives. Be sure to explain to the teens that these note cards are completely anonymous. They should not put their names on the cards, and no one besides the youth leaders leading the group will be looking at these, and then only to pray over them.

Note: It's a MUST that you use discretion with these cards. Don't lay them in a place where someone who is not supposed to read them could have access to them, and do not share the content with anyone, unless there is some legitimate and intentional reason (such as in the case of the threat of harm to a student). These are extremely sensitive areas that many teens will be bringing up, and your discretion will make the difference between a teen sharing about the lies he or she has believed, and not sharing. Lies are powerful things that we hold on to, and often bringing them into the light is the most important step in giving them up.

Instructions for leaders to give after passing out the cards:

★ **What we'd like you to do with the card you have is to write down three lies you've identified through this session that you had previously believed.**

★ **These are completely anonymous; we won't share the contents of these cards.**

★ **Listen to this list of Sample Lies to see if you relate to any of these. Or simply write the ones that come to your mind. (Review the list of Sample Lies with the group.)**

KEY POINTS FOR CLOSING

Give your students five minutes to work on their cards. Remind them to keep their note cards secret!

When your students are finished writing down their lies, let volunteers go around and discreetly collect the cards. A team member—preferably someone in authority over the meeting—can pray over the lies and pray for the group of teens. Ask specifically that God will break the ties that these lies have held on the teens' lives. Ask him to speak to each teen in the weeks to come about freedom in Christ. Ask him to give them a passion to learn and use his Word to defeat the lies of the enemy.

As a leader, it may be a good idea as you collect the cards to take a quick mental note of the most common lies, or of any potentially dangerous situations. Later you can make written notes for yourself so you can pray against the power of these lies on a regular basis.

After praying for the teens, dispose of the cards, symbolizing that God will help your students throw away the lies they've believed.

Or you can simply skip the step of collecting the cards and have the teens dispose of the cards themselves. Some ideas include:

★ **Burn the cards in a fire (you must be sure the fire is legal and safe) to represent the power of the lies being broken.**

★ **Let the students tear up their lie cards and throw them away.**

FOR SMALL GROUPS

In small groups, it often works well to have the leader take a quick look at the cards, and then tear them up one by one. This is a powerful representation that these lies can be broken in your students' lives.

(Note: To ensure the teens' privacy, be sure to dispose of the torn-up cards after the session. Again, burning them can be a good idea.)

FOR WEEKEND RETREATS

A weekend retreat is a great opportunity for kids to take a step back and view things from another perspective. Be sure to take advantage of this time in this way. Again, the fire disposal method can be especially powerful.

LEADER TIP
Expect different reactions during the closing session. Some students may be deeply moved, while others may respond more casually. Have a prayer team in place to help the students while they process their emotions.

LEADER TIP
If you choose to burn the note cards in a fire, after the students fill out the cards, take everyone outside. Explain that our God is a consuming fire (read Deuteronomy 4:24; this is very powerful), and by the power of the blood of Christ, we are set free from the lies of the enemy. Then let the teens put their lies into the fire. (Again, be sure the fire is safe, legal, and always monitored. After you're done, make sure the fire is completely extinguished.)

FOR CAMPS

Camp offers kids the chance to get away from outside influences and get a different view of their inner lives. And camp also offers easy access to a campfire! Sing some songs or have open sharing (never forced); this can be an incredibly powerful time. Then burn the note cards in the fire and close with prayer or an appropriate song.

THE REVOLUTION CONTINUES

Below are several suggestions for follow-up with your teens, using their favorite forms of communication. However, keep in mind that one of the best ways to continue the purity revolution is through the use of the *Culture Shock* survival guide for teens: the specially crafted companion to the Culture Shock event.

Here are a few sample text messages, Facebook updates, tweets, or e-mails you can use to connect with your group. (Shorten them as needed.) If your church's website has a youth page, use that space as well. Use the media that you know will best connect with your students.

SAMPLE MESSAGES

- What lies are you believing? Be on guard! Read Ps 119:30.
- How many lies have you believed today? Read Prov 23:23.
- Check out Phil 4:13 today!
- Don't be deceived! Read 1 Cor 6:9 today.
- Don't let the enemy wrap you in lies! Matt 16:23.
- How many lies have you cut through today with the Word? John 8:32.
- Are you living like a world changer? Take the challenge! Read Mark 16:15.
- Where did your thoughts drift today? Read Col 3:2.
- Remember: Moviemakers have messages they want you to hear. 2 Cor 5:16.
- If Jesus were hanging out with you today, would you be embarrassed? Read 1 Cor 5:6.
- What does Ron Luce's quote in the *Culture Shock* survival guide mean to you?
- Remember how God spoke to you? Now let's live like it! Ps 143:5. (Post as a caption with a photo from the last session.)
- Have you used your sword today? Eph 6:17.
- Have you been reading your *Culture Shock* survival guide? What do you think about doing a media fast?
- Stand up for right, even if you stand alone. Look up Ps 62:2.
- "Guard your heart, for everything you do flows from it." Prov 4:23.

BUILDING THE BRIDGE

Youth leaders often come to us asking how to get parents "up to speed" on what was taught during Culture Shock. Use the ideas below to connect with parents to make sure they know what their kids are being told regarding purity, relationships, dating, media, and the many other things we cover. We've also included ideas on helping parents connect with their teens about these issues. For more resources, including weekly parent updates and key resource recommendations, visit us online at www.generationsofvirtue.org.

OVERVIEW OF CINDERELLA LIED, SUPERMAN DIED

Today's media is bombarding your kids like never before. The influence that it has is immense, ranging from who your teens imitate, to how they talk, to what they wear and who they choose to date. The problem is, media and technology often draw our teens away from God instead of toward him by lying to them and giving them a false perception of reality and truth.

We took a significant amount of time to explain to your kids how to discern what messages are buried in media. We showed them movie clips from some popular films and talked about the lies transmitted through those scenes, helping them to learn how to view entertainment with a discerning eye. If they can understand the objectives behind the media, they will be better able to pick out the lies that the enemy is trying to tell them.

After completing the movie clips, we encouraged the teens to recognize the lies that are at work in their lives. We asked them to write down (anonymously) three lies on note cards—false messages that they have believed.

Some common lies that we often hear from teens are: 1) My parents don't love me; 2) My parents love my brother/sister more; 3) God doesn't care about who I am or what I do. Does this come as a surprise to you? It did to us! But it confirmed what experts have been saying and what we have known all along: Parents, you matter! You have incredible impact, influence, and authority in your teens' lives. They NEED you. They NEED to be loved and encouraged by you. Don't let this window of opportunity pass you by!

After the teens were able to identify the lies that they believed, we destroyed the note cards to symbolize the breaking of the power of lies in their lives.

FIVE GREAT DISCUSSION POINTS FOR PARENTS AND TEENS

1. How has media shaped the way you view yourself? When you watch shows (like sports, reality shows, and so on), how do you walk away feeling? Do you ever feel like you're not good enough the way you are?

2. How has media affected the way you view relationships? What about the way you view sex? (Parents: If you haven't talked to your teens about sex, now is the time to do so!)

3. Parents, talk about some lies you believed as a teen. Then ask: Are you able to filter out the lies you hear? Which ones are harder for you to keep out of your head? If you're comfortable with it, will you share with me the three lies you wrote down on the note card?

4. Since a lot of lies come through the media—things like songs, TV, music, movies, and the Internet—what are some things our family can do to protect each other from these messages? Let's think of three practical things we can do in our home.

5. What is the most significant point that you took away from the event?

CONNECT: AN ACTIVITY FOR PARENTS AND TEENS

To continue the lessons learned in "Cinderella Lied, Superman Died," we want you to evaluate your family's media habits/intake this week. How much time do you spend as a family *without* input from media? As individuals, how much time are you spending *with* media? It may be helpful to make a chart for each family member to fill in for one week.

At the end of the week, arrange a time for your whole family to discuss media use in your home. Discuss what should be the appropriate viewing standards for your family. These media standards should cover the following: movies, music, TV, Internet viewing, video games, and more.

Write or print out your family's standards, and post them around the house, especially next to the computer, by the TV, and near the stereo. You could also make digital files of the standards and put them up as pictures on your portable devices, phones, and other screens.

Here is one example of a family standards list:

> # OUR FAMILY'S MEDIA GUIDE
>
> **1.** We will only watch TV and movies that don't dishonor God.
>
> **2.** As a family, we choose to shield our hearts, minds, and bodies against things that are impure. This means that we choose not to watch or listen to media that encourages sexual behavior or includes explicit content or anything else that might cause us to stumble.
>
> **3.** As a family, we want to fulfill our God-given destiny. We commit to limiting the time we spend watching TV or movies, listening to music, playing video games, and surfing the Internet to one hour a day (total) to ensure that we have more than enough time to accomplish the things that really matter.
>
> **4.** We are committed to purity. If we see or hear anything that would compromise our purity, such as pornographic content, we will turn off whatever we were doing and go tell Dad and/or Mom right away.
>
> **5.** As parents, Dad and Mom commit to modeling appropriate viewing standards for our own lives and for the entire family.
>
> **6.** As a family, we don't want to be caught off guard by our movie choices, so if we are going to the theater, we will read a Christian media outlet's review on the movie first.
>
> **7.** If we are ever placed in a compromising situation regarding media when we are not at home, we will call Dad and/or Mom and let them know, "I need a ride home."

Whatever you come up with, make sure that it is tailored to your family's needs. Establishing clear standards for your family's media intake is critical in helping your teens develop safe and healthy media choices.

PLUG IN

Youth leaders should be sure to e-mail parents to communicate with them about what their teens have been discussing and learning. Feel free to send parents the Overview of the session and the Five Great Discussion Points. Introduce them to the idea of the Connect activity as well. Include your contact information so parents can reach you if they have questions.

Make use of Facebook updates, Twitter messages, texts, and e-mail to send messages of encouragement and connection to parents. If they don't use any of these forms of communication, find out what works best for them (a phone call, brief meetings). Just keep the communication lines open!

SAMPLE MESSAGES

- Had a great time with your teen! Want to know more about what they learned? Check your e-mail!
- Your kids are learning how to discern the lies of the enemy vs. the awesome truth of God's Word! We're learning together! Are you learning too?
- We're setting the captives free in this event! Don't forget to ask your teen about it!
- Have you used the Five Discussion Points yet?
- Be sure to do the parent/teen activity sometime this week!
- Help your teen break the power of lies. Pray for your teen before school today. Speak God's Word into his/her life.

- Rent a movie tonight to watch with your teen. Help expose lies that the entertainment industry might be trying to feed us. (For example: Is the main character involved in terrible behavior? Is that real life? Do their choices reflect actual consequences?)
- How many of you have seen a difference in your teen this week? Message me back and let me know how it's going!
- Need good recommendations to keep up with your kids? Check out www.generationsofvirtue.org for a lot more!

BRACE FOR IMPACT

This session is designed to help teens handle the media tsunami that faces them each and every day. The point here is not to tell them that all kinds of media and technology are bad—not even close! Instead, we want to help teens realize that technology can and should be used to expand the reach of the kingdom of God and spread the gospel message.

We at Generations of Virtue have seen so many good things come about through media and technology. Millions of people have been exposed to the message of Christ through music, blogs, tweets and posts, satellite TV shows, and virtual churches in online games. Christians are being discipled through podcasts, MP3 resources, and text messaging.

But just like every other good thing, the use of communication devices and technology can be twisted by the enemy. That is why it's vital to be aware of the dangers of porn, trashy music, inappropriate social networking, and explicit or violent shows. The goal is to help teens not only avoid harmful media but also use media to advance God's kingdom. As you work through this session, encourage your teens to use the tools provided in the *Culture Shock* survival guide to keep track of their time, especially concerning media usage.

In "Brace for Impact," your students will plan and act out skits based on scenarios relating to media and the use of technology. The cool part about this is that you can do these scenes in a variety of ways, and your teens will get to participate more than in any other session. No matter if you're leading a small group, large group, weekend retreat, or camp, the session will be composed of four parts:

* **explaining the instructions and rules**
* **having your students perform the skits**
* **giving your teens time to prepare their skits**
* **and discussing what the teens learned**

This session brings out the best in teens. We've seen it embraced wherever we go around the world because of its lighthearted and often hysterical approach to very real issues in our society today. Here's something else we often see: the formatting of the skits allows even the shy kids in your group to shine.

Before you dive into this session, take some time to:

* **READ—Read through the session and the Scriptures that are suggested throughout. Some helpful passages to look at are: Exodus 18:20; Proverbs 4:23; Matthew 5:13-16; Luke 8:17; 1 Corinthians 10:12; Ephesians 5:1-20; 1 Thessalonians 5:4-11. Read the surrounding verses or chapters of these passages so you are aware of the context.**

* **WATCH—In the time leading up to your session or event, watch out for specific examples of times when the use of media and technology has been twisted to serve the enemy's purposes. Having these examples fresh in your mind may be helpful as you lead your group.**

* **PRAY—Ask God for wisdom for yourself and your fellow leaders. Pray for humility and patience as you lead discussions with your teens. Pray for specific girls and guys you know who need to hear this message.**

BREAKING IT DOWN

"Brace for Impact" is one of the Culture Shock sessions for which we suggest allotting a little extra time. Your teens will be performing skits, and in addition to the performance time (we advise keeping the performances to two minutes only), you also need to allow for preparation and discussion time.

This session could be done in many different ways, depending on the size of

LEADER TIP

Even though you tell the teens to take two minutes for their skits, it's an unwritten rule that they will take longer. Tell them "two minutes," but with your discussion points, plan on five to seven minutes for each group.

your group and the time you have available. Here are some breakdown options for your large or small group:

1. Use this as a longer event by breaking it into three sessions:

★ **Session One: Give an overview and explain the scenarios. Divide the teens into groups (see Prepping the Session). Give the groups twenty to thirty minutes of skit preparation time. Then, as time permits, call on one or two groups to perform their skits. Be sure to take time to share the Key Discussion Points after each skit.**

★ **Session Two: Allow five to ten minutes to refresh their memories of their skits. (You may also have students who are not able to make it to all the sessions, so make adjustments to fill all the roles. Youth leaders can fill in as needed.) All the groups who did not perform in the first session can then do their skits. Again, be sure to allow discussion time after every scenario.**

★ **Session Three: Keeping students in the same skit groups, let them pick a challenge (see The Challenge section later in this chapter) to do for this session. It's a good idea to make sure that the teens stay on the property at which you're meeting, but give them freedom to use various locations around that property, if possible.**

2. For two sessions, try it this way:

★ **Session One: Give an overview and explain the scenarios. Once the teens have been separated into groups (see Prepping the Session), give them twenty to thirty minutes of skit prep time. Let half of the groups perform their skits, and be sure to share the discussion points in between performances.**

★ **Session Two: Let the remaining groups perform their skits— again, don't forget the discussion points! For the remainder of the session, let them pick a challenge to do (see The Challenge section later in this chapter). It's a good idea to make sure that the teens stay on the property at which you're meeting, but give them freedom to use various locations around that property, if possible.**

3. Use this as one big session: Give an overview and explain the scenarios. Once the teens have been separated into groups (see Prepping the Session), give them twenty to thirty minutes of skit prep time. Let all the groups perform their skits. Be sure to share the discussion points between each skit. As a closing, encourage the teens to do one of the recommended challenges (see The Challenge section later in this chapter) to seal what they have learned at the event.

THE MAIN EVENT

O nce you've decided how to organize your sessions, gathered your equipment and leaders—and your teens!—pray together and get ready to enter performance mode.

ACTIVITY: PLAYING THE PART

Unlike what happens in other Culture Shock events, this activity takes up the whole event time.

PREPPING THE SESSION

For this activity, you'll find that some teens love to get into acting out the scenes, and others shy away. A helpful way to get everyone involved is to offer people the chance to play the role of props or to be narrators. Don't worry if a few of your groups need an extra push to get them going. If a particular group is having a difficult time getting started, a youth leader or two can join the group to liven it up.

LEADER TIP
A fun idea is to allow your teens to record their skits and/or comments on what they've learned during the event. If you decide to do this, make sure you have enough video recording devices for the number of groups, and make sure you have a good way of projecting the videos so your whole group can see.

You'll need to break the teens into small groups for this session. How many groups you have will depend on how many participants are in the session and how much time you have. The skits turn out best if each group has between five and twelve teens.

You will give each group a prewritten scenario relating to some kind of technology: the Internet, iPods and music, cell phones, video games, TV and movies. After some preparation time, the teens will have two minutes to perform a skit, music video, commercial, or song based on the prewritten plot they were given. After each group performs, leaders will communicate some discussion points about the particular issue brought up in the skit (see Key Discussion Points after each of the example plots provided later in this chapter).

Before the session, you'll need to put together group envelopes with the prewritten plots and the activity rules in them (see The Rules). Then place group number signs throughout the meeting area. You will break the teens into groups by giving each person a card (or paper or sticker) with a number on it. You can either leave numbers on the chairs or pass them out as the teens enter the room or even during the session itself, if you have a smaller group.

Spread the groups out a good distance from each other, as they'll need space to prepare their skits.

Make sure to provide the groups with any materials they might need to prepare for their performances. Items could include: paper, pens, markers, posterboard, and recording devices (video cameras or other).

LEADER TIP

When you're passing out the cards or otherwise breaking the teens into groups, be sure that you attempt to put close friends into different groups. We've learned from experience: these skits turn out best if the teens are broken out of their normal cliques. So for example, if you're passing out numbers at the door for a large group, arrange them in 1-2-3-4-5 order, so friends walking in together will end up in different groups.

OPEN UP

Here's a suggestion for opening the session with prayer:

Lord, we pray that you would direct this session according to your will. We thank you for all the forms of communication that are available to us. Please show us how to use media and technology to advance your kingdom. If there are areas where we have abused the gifts you've given us, show us how to escape the traps we've fallen into. We pray you'd be with us as we learn how to honor you with technology. In Jesus' name, amen.

LEADER TIP

Sometimes teens may act out inappropriate scenes a little too realistically, and they can end up crossing some lines. Don't be afraid to step in and censor when necessary! A less stern and very fun way to censor is to make a poster that says something funny— maybe "Buzzzz!" or "Not Happening!"—or has a big red X on it. You or one of the other leaders can hold the sign up in front of the group if you don't like where the skit is going. This lightens the mood for the other teens while also getting the point across that the group's performance needs to change direction.

THE RULES

When you're explaining the activity, it's important to go over the rules with your students. If you're equipped with a projector and screen (or blank wall, white sheet, etc.), put the rules up on a slide show so all the teens can read them as you go over them. They'll have a copy of the rules in their group envelopes as well, but it's always best to go over them together at the beginning. The topics brought up in the scenarios are meant to address common issues teens struggle with in areas such as pornography, social networking, texting, video games, and more.

Say something like this to your students to kick this activity off: In this session, your group will be preparing a visual presentation about teen media issues. Your job is to:

★ **Create a TWO-minute skit, song, music video, or commercial based on the plot you were given. Remember to read**

The Rules before you begin.

★ **Present what you create in front of everyone later in this session.**

Goal: The point of these skits is to help you and your friends develop a plan so that when you are in these situations, you'll know what to do!

OK, here are The Rules:

> **1.** Read the plot out LOUD to your audience before the presentation.
>
> **2.** Include EVERYONE in your group, either as a character or as a prop. Use your imagination: group members can play lots of inanimate things, like a computer or a chair or a TV screen.
>
> **3.** Keep your presentations CLEAN! No profanities or obscene behavior.
>
> **4.** SPEAK loudly and clearly so that everyone can hear you.
>
> **5.** Be CREATIVE and HAVE FUN!

THE SCENES

Set a designated time that you want to give each group to plan their skits, such as twenty or thirty minutes—whatever works best for your group. Make sure the teams know their designated prep time and stick to it.

Give your groups time to go after it, help them if help is needed, and then call the groups back together for the performances.

The following are example scenes for the teens to act out. If there are more plots listed than you have

LEADER TIP
Feel free to write your own plots as you see the need. Maybe there's a particular issue you notice a group of your teens dealing with—a skit might be an excellent opportunity to help change some perspectives in your group!

groups, pick scenarios from a variety of topics. We've listed discussion points to go along with each plot. These are for you to talk about after each group has presented their skit. Where appropriate, add in your own stories to share with the teens.

 SCENE 1: Candid Camera

TOPIC: Social networking

SETTING: Dressing room at the mall

MESSAGE: Everything you post online is permanent and everyone can see it!

PLOT: You're with a group of friends at the mall, and your friends start trying on clothes that they wouldn't normally be allowed to wear. One of your friends starts joking around and taking pictures with a cell phone. On your way home, without telling you, this friend uploads all of them online. By the time you get to church on Sunday, your parents, pastors, and friends have seen the pictures. Now you're totally busted.

What should you have done? And what will you do now?

KEY DISCUSSION POINTS

★ **Every file on the Internet can live forever. You may think deleting those trashy pictures off your social network page will cause them to go away, but they can resurface years later when you least expect it.**

★ **You never know when someone will whip out a phone and upload a pic of you that you DO NOT want anyone to see—especially your parents. Be aware of cell phone cameras.**

★ **A good rule of thumb: If you wouldn't want it shown on a big screen at church, don't put it on the Internet. And if you don't want it on the Internet, don't get in this situation in the first place!**

★ **Remember: As a Christian, you are an example to those around you. Check out Matthew 5:13-16.**

SCENE 2: Blog Bashing—Busted!

TOPIC: Blogging

SETTING: Your friend's bedroom

MESSAGE: Blogging is for your personal interests, not for bashing on other people.

PLOT: You and a group of friends get busted by one of your teachers for cheating on a math test. Your friend goes home and blogs about how messed up your teacher is and ends up saying some pretty ugly things about him. Your teacher and your parents find the blog post, and when they demand an explanation for all the trash talking, you stand up for your friend instead of backing up what is right.

What should you have done? What will you do now?

KEY DISCUSSION POINTS

★ If you can't say something nice, don't say it in a blog. A blog is not for bashing people. Don't ever do this to teachers, coaches, pastors, leaders, friends, or anyone! You might assume this is your private conversation, but anyone *on earth* can find this. Even when you hide it.

★ Put content on your blog that's going to encourage other people to grow in their faith in God. Take an honest look at the content and evaluate whether it meets this standard. Writing blog posts is a great way to use technology to spread the amazing truth about Jesus. You never know who might stumble onto your blog at any given time and find something that is really useful or inspiring. A blog can be an amazing platform to impact thousands of people.

★ When you're writing in your blog, take your cue from Moses! Check out Exodus 18:20.

SCENE 3: Real Friends Go Virtual—Right?

TOPIC: Social networking

SETTING: Your bedroom

MESSAGE: Investing so much time in shallow relationships can leave you without any actual friends.

PLOT: You and your "friends" are ALWAYS online. Every day begins and ends with texts, online chats, status updates, and new posts. At first this seemed cool, but now you all realize that those online connections and conversations can't fill the need for deep, meaningful relationships. And you've even started feeling awkward in face-to-face interactions.

How could you have avoided this situation? What can you guys do now?

KEY DISCUSSION POINTS

★ **Virtual vs. real relationships: Virtual relationships take away the blush factor—things you're not bold enough to say in person will come out through social networking, chatting, text messages, and other forms of social media. More often than not, you'll end up saying things you regret.**

★ **God designed normal, face-to-face interaction for a reason.**

Friendship is a training ground for life on many levels.

★ **Get real: Seek face-to-face relationships and don't be afraid to pull the plug on your online accounts, or at least take a break to clear your head for a while.**

★ **Read 1 Thessalonians 5:11 for more on this!**

 SCENE 4: I <3 You, I <3 You Not

TOPIC: Texting

SETTING: The youth room at church

MESSAGE: Talking via technology can be really harmful when you are not careful.

PLOT: You and a girl from church have been friends since you were a little boy. But the "just friends" stage began wearing off and you began liking each other. She recently admitted to you over text that she liked you, and you've been messaging back and forth every day, saying things you wouldn't say if she were standing there in front of you. But now your friendship is crumbling, and you totally regret letting it go so far.

What should you do now?

★ **Don't rely on technology when you want to get to know someone. Just because you're connected with someone at a virtual level does not mean that you are really good friends. It's still important to have face-to-face interaction on a regular basis.**

★ **Never base romantic relationships on texts, chats, or social networking. Seeds of misunderstanding grow into relationships that are based on empty words and not a sure foundation.**

★ **Bonding absolutely can happen over social media—so it is really important to guard what you say. (More on this will be discussed in the "Fearless Purity" session.) Check out Proverbs 4:23 for more.**

 SCENE 5: Can't Believe She Sent *That*!

TOPIC: Sexting

SETTING: Coffeehouse

MESSAGE: Know what to do if a bad pic gets messaged to you.

PLOT: You and a group of guy friends are meeting for Bible study at your favorite coffee hangout when a girl from work messages you a pic of herself in a really inappropriate outfit. It totally catches you off guard, and your friends want to know why in the world you're suddenly so speechless and shocked.

What do you do now?

KEY DISCUSSION POINTS

★ **If someone sends you an inappropriate pic, DELETE IT right away. Don't save it for later. Don't show it around and then delete it. Just get rid of it immediately.**

★ **Whenever anyone communicates with you in an inappropriate way, be sure to let one of your leaders know what happened so you can stay accountable.**

★ **This is a situation in which God is calling you to stand apart. You can refuse to text or respond to pics that treat people like objects to be used by others. Rather, you can make a statement that people aren't objects but a critical part of God's creation. Read 1 Thessalonians 5:5, 6 for follow-up.**

SCENE 6: Just One More Level!

TOPIC: Video games

SETTING: Your aunt's living room

MESSAGE: If you're spending too much time gaming, other areas of your life are going to suffer.

PLOT: It's been happening for about three weeks now. Every day after you finish your schoolwork, you head over to your aunt's house and play video games for hours. Now you're totally hooked and spend every waking moment thinking about or playing these games, and your sleep, grades, and friendships are taking a backseat to entertainment. You want to change, but aren't sure how.

What should you do?

KEY DISCUSSION POINTS

★ **It's easy to lose ourselves in virtual worlds. We know that real life can be really hard, and sometimes it feels like more than we can take. But the truth is that God has designed your reality to teach you life lessons that you aren't going to be able to learn anywhere else.**

★ **The enemy is out to steal away the time of this generation. It's important to realize that the time you spend playing video games is time you can't ever get back. Check out Ephesians 5:15, 16.**

SCENE 7: M for Mature

TOPIC: Video games

SETTING: Your bedroom

MESSAGE: Know what to do if porn shows up in your games.

PLOT: You and some friends have been waiting on the newest video game for months. It finally comes out, and you're the first to get it, so everyone heads over to your house. But as you're playing, you realize that this game is way more obscene than the previous version. Pictures of sex, drugs, and violence keep popping up. You want to keep playing, and there aren't any adults around, so no one would know what you and your friends are seeing. But something in you is urging you to shut it off.

What should you do?

KEY DISCUSSION POINTS

* Even though you may be alone, that doesn't mean that what you do in secret does not come into the light. God's Word promises us that eventually everything will come into the light. Who you are when no one is watching is who you really are. Check out Luke 8:17.

* If you struggle with games—whether it be the content of the games or the amount of time you spend playing them, or both—make it a point to only play when someone else is around or playing with you. Stay accountable to people you know who have the same or higher standards than you do when it comes to gaming.

* Especially if you struggle with content in games, place your game unit in a high-traffic area of your home, where someone just walking by will be able to see what you're playing.

 SCENE 8: Should I Stay or Should I Go Now?

TOPIC: Movies

SETTING: The movie theater

MESSAGE: What to do if you're caught off guard by a movie's content.

PLOT: You and your friends are hanging out after school and decide to see a movie. The previews seemed totally fine, but after the movie gets started, you realize it's A LOT worse than what you expected. You want to get up and leave, but then you'd be left with no friends and no ride home, so you just stay and ride it out. Long after the movie is finished, even though you want to stop thinking about *that* scene, you can't. You seriously wish you had never gone to the movie in the first place.

What could you have done differently? Will this affect what you do in the same situation next time?

KEY DISCUSSION POINTS

* We know it can be seriously difficult to walk out of a movie where all your friends are. We know they'll laugh and ask what in the world you're doing. But do you know what is a lot more difficult? Going to your youth pastor two months later needing help because you still can't get that scene out of your head—and now you spend every night fantasizing about what you saw. Trust us—it's worth it to walk out.

* No one ever said that standing up for what you believe in is an easy thing to do. But chances are, if you make the stand once, you won't be put in that position again. And if your friends are truly friends, then they will

respect your decision, even if they choose to stay. Your job is just to stay true to your commitment to honor God. Check out Ephesians 5:11!

★ Remember not to let pride ruin your chance to be a good example to others. Don't judge your friends if they stay behind. But do answer honestly if they ask why you left.

SCENE 9: Isn't Everyone Watching It?

TOPIC: Television

SETTING: The TV room or home theater room

MESSAGE: Find out what a huge impact TV can have on a person's life.

PLOT: Thursday night rolls around and you spend it the way you always do—in front of the TV watching your absolute favorite show. You don't think much about the content at the time. I mean, it's TV, right?

On Sunday morning your youth pastor starts talking about how much TV affects us, especially when most shows are filled with lust, sex, and violence. He challenges you to take a media fast and refrain from watching anything that you wouldn't watch with Jesus sitting next to you. While you agreed with him at the time, and even promised to stop watching that stuff, when you get home you *really* want to turn on the TV.

How do you keep the promise you made?

KEY DISCUSSION POINTS

★ If you're in the habit of watching a certain TV show, schedule something else during that time so you won't be tempted to turn it on. Find something else to do, like hanging out with a friend, reading a book, or asking to be put on the schedule at work—anything to keep you away from the TV! You might be surprised by what God can do with that time.

★ If you're being prompted by God to do something—whether it's a TV fast or something else—he'll give you everything you

need to follow through. Make a commitment before God to avoid anything that you're not supposed to watch. Times like this are excellent—and necessary—opportunities to learn how to rely on him.

★ For encouragement to keep going, read Matthew 6:17, 18.

SCENE 10: When You Play with Fire

TOPIC: Internet filtering

SETTING: Your living room

MESSAGE: Internet filtering is one of the best ways to keep you—and those around you—accountable.

PLOT: After school, your normal routine is to go home and start your schoolwork so you can eat dinner with the fam when they all get home (that's awesome!). Usually it's harmless: you stay busy, keep out of trouble, and generally mind your work. But this particular day you find yourself with a few spare minutes and end up wandering onto websites you know you shouldn't be looking at.

How could you have avoided this? And now that you've seen those images, what should you do?

KEY DISCUSSION POINTS

★ We all need to be held accountable—no matter who we are or what we've done. No one is exempt. Check out 1 Corinthians 10:12.

★ Filtering and accountability software are excellent ways to let others keep tabs on what you're doing on the Internet.

★ Your character is determined by the choices you make when no one is watching. What characteristics do you want to define you? Remember: who you are on the inside is way more important than who you are (or who people *think* you are) on the outside. The choices you make are defining your behavior and how you act. The way you spend your time determines how you live your life. Learn more about this in the *Culture Shock* survival guide.

SCENE 11: That's Not Really My Style

TOPIC: Cyberbullying

SETTING: Biology class

MESSAGE: Know how to respond to cyberbullying.

PLOT: A few weeks ago, a girl in your bio class made a few bad comments on a social network about the popular crowd at school. Since then, everyone has been telling horrible lies about her all over text and the

Internet. A guy from your class even took a terrible picture of her and posted it online and sent it to the entire school. You feel bad for this girl, but are afraid that if you stand up for her, you'll be targeted next.

What should you do?

KEY DISCUSSION POINTS

★ The Golden Rule says: "Treat others as you would like to be treated." If you're the one bullying, you may feel like king or queen of the hill right now, but God has a way of taking us out of our comfy situations in order to teach us a lesson. You may find yourself at a new school or new town or new social group and end up on the bottom of the pile. How would you like to be treated in this situation?

★ If you're on the receiving end of the bullying, this is an opportune time to find your strength and your worth in the Lord. What does he say about you?

Who does he say you are? Don't listen to people who don't know you like he does. He is the one who defines us—not our peers. If the situation is really bad or abusive, let an adult know ASAP. Don't be afraid to tell someone what's going on.

★ Even if you feel like you personally can't stand up on your own for a person who is getting bullied, tell an adult so that he or she can intervene. Often, adults don't see the things that you can see.

★ Remember how special you are to God! Check out Zechariah 2:8.

 SCENE 12: I'm Not Hearing This!!

TOPIC: Song lyrics and artists

SETTING: The car

MESSAGE: It's so important to listen to the words of a song, not just the beat. And to know who you are listening to!

PLOT: Lately you've been paying closer attention to the lyrics in the songs you like on the radio. You realize that what these people are singing about is actually pretty terrible! Not to mention the artists themselves—most of them are known for living pretty trashy lifestyles. But now it seems like no matter what you do, you can't get away from this kind of music—it's everywhere! In the car, with your friends, at the mall, in the cafeteria—all over the place!

What are some things you can do to avoid having these lyrics running through your mind?

★ Be aware of what you're listening to and avoid explicit music whenever you can. This might even mean not going into your favorite store or coffee shop if they're blasting questionable stuff.

★ According to a study published in the *Journal of the American Medical Association*, "1 in 5 US adolescents 12 to 19 years old demonstrated hearing loss."[1] This result, from a group studied in 2005–2006, was a one-third increase from results obtained from 1988–1994. Exposure to noise pollution was listed as one of the causes. Noise—not just loud music—bombards many of us 24/7. And much of it comes directly against our eardrums through our own earbuds. Our suggestion? Listen through speakers (at a reasonable level) whenever possible instead of through earbuds. And sometimes . . . just turn it off!

★ Listening to worship music and spending time worshipping is one of the best ways to fall deeply in love with God. Download some worship music on your MP3 player and listen to something that lifts your mood and talks about hope, strength, and peace, not something that tears you down. Check out Ephesians 5:17-20.

YOUR VIEW

For any of the skits, list other discussion points that you see as important to communicate to your group.

FOR SMALL GROUPS

This is an excellent session for small groups because everyone can participate. You may consider having the leaders perform a skit or two—either in their own group or mixed in with the teens. It's a lot of fun! Since you may not have enough teens to perform all the prewritten plots, be sure to pick the ones that are more pertinent to your group.

FOR WEEKEND RETREATS

You have the option of giving the teens more time to prepare their skits. If you're diligent about putting teens in groups they don't normally hang out in, this is an excellent chance to get them connecting with people other than their usual friends. They can take free time between scheduled sessions to prepare their skits and possibly pull in some props.

LEADER TIP
Aren't crazy about some—or any—of these skits? Feel free to write your own! Whatever your group is into, use this session to address the issues that your group faces the most.

FOR CAMPS

Similar to weekend retreats, you can give teens more time to prepare their skits, and you can also use the opportunity to break up the normal cliques and get the teens hanging out with new groups. We love the idea of performing the skits in the middle of the week for camps. They provide an awesome time of getting connected and breaking up tight groups, all while laughing and having a great time together! Also, these skits create awesome memories and lots of conversation starters for the rest of the week.

After the last group has presented, make sure you've left plenty of time to discuss all the performances together and to present The Challenge (see below). Let groups comment on each other's scenes. This can make for great, wide-ranging discussion!

THE CHALLENGE

Close the session by giving your teens a challenge. The whole point of the session is to help teenagers think of ways they can use technology to build up God's kingdom instead of their own agendas. Advancing God's kingdom needs to begin in their hearts and minds and then move outward to the world around them. Encourage your teens to explore these ideas through the use of their *Culture Shock* survival guides.

Communicate to your students that this is their challenge. You also want to encourage your teens that if they're struggling with any of the areas mentioned in the scenes, they should find a leader and talk about it.

Close this session in prayer, specifically asking God to move and show your students where and how they need to change their media and technology habits and how they can use technology for his purposes.

Challenge ideas:

★ **Teens could make video podcasts or diaries that follow up the message they heard this week, or on other topics that they're learning about.**

★ **Encourage your teens to volunteer to make video announcements for your congregation.**

★ **For your more tech-savvy teens, encourage them to offer their time to make media presentations for pastors or other speakers at your church.**

★ **Volunteer some of your teens to put together a movie or video from a recent mission trip. Even if they didn't go, they can offer to make a follow-up video or slide show.**

★ **Get a teen worship team to record an album.**

★ **Teens could blog about what God is showing and teaching them this week/month.**

★ **If your teens had a great time with these skits, why not keep it going? Write your own plots and have your teens film the skits on their own; then have a viewing party together at youth group. Hand out prizes for the most creative, best overall, and more. Make it a mini-Oscars night!**

★ **Challenge your teens to work through their *Culture Shock* survival guides with a group of friends. They could start a Bible study to encourage those around them to stand pure.**

YOUR VIEW

List other challenge ideas you may have:

THE REVOLUTION CONTINUES

This session has the potential to really convict teens about the choices they're making with media and the way they use technology. It's important for you and your fellow leaders to be available after the session to counsel or help in other ways in these areas. For example, if a teen has identified pornography as an issue in his or her life, that person will need a lot of ongoing support. We've found some excellent resources on the issue:

★ **Tactics, by Fred Stoeker with Mike Yorkey**

★ **Every Young Man's Battle, by Stephen Arterburn and Fred Stoeker with Mike Yorkey** (A word of caution: We've found this book best suited for teens who are at the point of addiction to porn or sex, rather than for those not at that point. Some of the stories and examples in the book are explicit because the authors are trying to get young men to see how destructive these addictions are. Please review this book before giving it to a member of your group.)

★ **Every Young Woman's Battle, by Shannon Ethridge and Stephen Arterburn**

★ **What Are You Waiting For? by Dannah Gresh**

Encourage your teens to seek out accountability for things such as their Internet habits. There are tons of free and/or inexpensive filtering software that can help people to stay accountable. Check out www.generationsofvirtue.org for our latest recommendations.

Also, remember that *Culture Shock: A Survival Guide for Teens* does a fantastic job of encouraging teens to hold to a high media standard, so be sure to have your teens check it out today!

Here are a few sample text messages, Facebook updates, tweets, or e-mails you can use to connect with your group. (Shorten them as needed.) If your church's website has a youth page, use that space as well. Use the media that you know will best connect with your students.

SAMPLE MESSAGES

• What are some ideas you've come up with to use technology to advance God's kingdom?

• How are your thoughts doing? 2 Cor 10:5

• Use this to fight temptation: 1 Cor 10:13

• Have you made a covenant with your eyes? Job 31:1

• Poll: What do you spend the most

time on? FB, texting, TV, movies? Text me your answer back!

- Have you identified one of your time-wasters? What is it?
- Poll: Which skit was the funniest? most impacting? Had the best acting? Text an answer back!

- Poll: What was your favorite part of this meeting/weekend/camp/_____?
- Heard any good worship music lately? What have you been listening to?
- What do you think about what you've been reading in your *Culture Shock* survival guide this week?

BUILDING THE BRIDGE

Brace for Impact is quite possibly one of the most necessary events for parents to be informed about. Many parents know little or nothing about how their kids are using media in their everyday lives. Technology is so vastly different from when today's parents were teenagers; some of these moms and dads (or other guardians) don't realize how detrimental certain types of media have become—the same types of media that are considered vital, especially by our teenagers. Also, because of the sensitive issues that can come up during the discussion of media, it would be a good idea for youth leaders to give parents a heads-up before the event even begins. Then make a point to connect with parents after the event by using the information that follows.

Don't underestimate this fact: you may be the only one who has the ability to speak into parents' lives regarding this important subject. Whether it's through a parents' meeting, an e-mail, or some other form of connecting, be sure you communicate the important points discussed here.

OVERVIEW OF BRACE FOR IMPACT

"Brace for Impact" is a skit-based event where teens were put into common, yet compromising, fictional circumstances regarding media and then asked: "If you were faced with this situation, what would you do?" Our goal through this event was to help teens safeguard themselves against the dangers of today's media: cell phones, music, Internet, gaming, and more.

Often, teens get into trouble with media—such as sexting their friends, stumbling onto pornographic websites, or watching an inappropriate movie—because they don't have a plan in place. If they aren't equipped to know how to respond when these sorts of issues come up, they'll be caught off guard and will be more likely to give in to peer pressure instead of falling back on God's game plan.

The enemy sells harmful media as nothing more than entertainment. The messages presented through media help to shape the next generation and influence how they view life, love, and relationships. The producers and artists contributing to this entertainment have their own agendas, and sometimes their objectives go way beyond amusement.

But still, the most important influences on teens' lives come from their families. You as parents have the power and the privilege of shaping these young persons through the choices and habits that you engage in at home. Only you can pour into your teen's decision-making process on a daily basis through your example, through your conversations, and through your love. Don't let the enemy tell you anything different!

FIVE GREAT DISCUSSION POINTS FOR PARENTS AND TEENS

1. Name your favorite: a) TV show, b) movie, c) band, d) song. What do you like about each of these? Can you think of a quote or a part of a song that really means something to you? Why is it meaningful? Is there anything in these shows or songs you really disagree with? What is it, and why?

2. If Jesus were sitting next to you when you watched your favorite shows or listened to those songs, is there anything you would change? If our pastor came over for dinner and that TV show was playing in the background, would you be embarrassed?

3. Songs, movies, TV, and the Internet have a way of shaping our view of reality and what we believe to be true. When you look at your favorite characters and artists, are they the type of people you want to shape your life? Why or why not?

4. Are you willing to make some changes in your life, such as removing negative media influences? How will you do this? How can I help you?

5. Let's say you're at a friend's house and someone puts in an R-rated movie filled with explicit scenes and terrible content—stuff you know you shouldn't be watching. What would you do? Has that already happened to you? How did you respond? What did you feel like doing? (Note to parents: When they answer these questions, do not freak out at the answers! If they made a poor choice in the past, help them understand how they can do things differently in the future.)

CONNECT: AN ACTIVITY FOR PARENTS AND TEENS

Sometimes making changes in our media intake can be a difficult thing to do. Often we become attached to watching certain movies or shows, listening to songs, or surfing our favorite websites. But if these influences aren't godly, if they aren't helping us move forward, then they're hindering us. And in the long run, we don't want anything holding us back from the awesome plan and purpose that God has in store for our lives. So though it is difficult, our activity for parents and teens this week is this:

1. Take time to go through ALL your movies, music, TV shows, web history— everything media-related.

2. Whatever distracts from your commitment to God, whatever has been stealing time away from family life, whatever has been putting ungodly thoughts or images in your mind—get rid of it! Delete it, toss it out, put it up for sale—just get it out of your home. We know this might sound a little extreme, but if we are going to be in passionate pursuit of our incredible Savior, then we have to remove anything that hinders us from being like him. (Read Hebrews 12:1.)

3. Reward your efforts as a family by doing something fun together, like going hiking, bowling, or out to eat ice cream.

PLUG IN

Use the Overview of the session to update parents of teens on the event contents. Put this in an e-mail along with the Five Great Discussion Points and also introduce them to the idea of the Connect activity. Encourage parents to keep the momentum going. Be sure to include your contact information so that parents can reach you if they have any questions. Don't forget: jump on www.generationsofvirtue.org for tons of resources to equip parents, teens, and leaders to stand pure in our world today.

Make use of Facebook updates, Twitter messages, texts, and e-mail to send messages of encouragement and connection to the parents of the teens you work with. If they don't use any of these forms of communication, find out what works best for them (a phone call, brief meetings). Just keep the communication lines open!

SAMPLE MESSAGES

- This event helped your teen steer clear of the traps media throws at kids!
- Safeguard your teen—know the type of media he or she is watching and listening to.
- Had an awesome session with your teen today, learning how to make great choices regarding media!
- Face the facts: the largest consumers of pornography are teens between the ages of twelve and eighteen. What can you do to help protect your teen?
- Plan a media fast for your family. Do something together—go hiking, take a road trip, fix up the house, play some sports outside.
- It's not too late to get involved in your teen's media choices. You can have the greatest influence on your teen's life.
- Set a standard for your kids by getting rid of any inappropriate movies and music that you own.
- Find faith-based online reviews for movies, songs, or video games before getting them for your family.

PART THREE

THE POPULARITY CONTEST

This session revolves around popularity and the difficulties surrounding teens, including relationships with friends and more-than-friends. From our experience with thousands of teens worldwide, we've found that cliques within the church are just as prevalent as they are in schools, but it's a problem often overlooked. We hope to shed light on this reality and help teens see their tremendous value and purpose in the body of Christ.

Before you dive into this session, take some time to:

★ **READ—Read through the session, of course, but also spend time in the Scriptures suggested throughout. The main passages are: Psalm 133:1; Isaiah 13:11; Matthew 5:23, 24, 44, 45; 25:40; Luke 6:27-38, 45; Ephesians 4:32. Read the surrounding verses or chapters of these passages so you are aware of the context.**

★ **WATCH—In the time leading up to your session or event, watch out for specific examples of clique behavior, bullying, or other divisive habits among the**

teens you know. Also watch out for examples of this behavior seen on TV, in advertising, or in recent movies. Having these examples fresh in your mind may be helpful as you lead your group.

★ **PRAY—Ask God for wisdom for yourself and your fellow leaders. Pray for guidance and sensitivity as you lead discussions with your teens. Pray for specific girls and guys you know who need to hear this message.**

BREAKING IT DOWN

For camps and weekend retreats, it's possible to complete this session in one day. For large groups and small groups, "The Popularity Contest" can be extended to fill two weeks instead of just one sitting. Here are some breakdown options for your large or small group:

1. Use this as a longer event by breaking it into two sessions:

- ★ **Session One: Do the Tangled Mess activity and How Would You Respond?**

- ★ **Session Two: Come up with an icebreaker and recap some of the points from the previous session. Then go into the Darts activity. Finish with The Memorial Wall.**

2. Use this as a one-session event by slightly lengthening your entire session time, and taking less time discussing the How Would You Respond? scenarios.

Because of increased cyberbullying, we encourage you to consider having a "no Internet or cell phone" rule. (You could do this for all your Culture Shock sessions, but it would be good for this one in particular.) It may be a bit of work to enforce this. However, though the kids may not believe it—or like you for saying it!—it will not kill them to unplug for a while. This helps get the teens focused and truly away from all their usual distractions, even for a short time. It also cuts down on the opportunity for anyone to take pictures or record parts of sensitive moments that may happen in this session (things that could later be used to tease someone through text or uploading items on the Internet). If you are planning a retreat or camp, think about access to cell phone or Internet signals. Sometimes there are unforeseen advantages to using a remote location!

LEADER TIP

This session offers an ideal opportunity to break up the usual cliques within your group. Divide up groups of friends or cliques into other cabins, rooms, or groups (depending on your venue) than they would normally want to be in. You'll have to hold your ground on this one; the kids do *not* like being split up. But trust us, it's worth it!

THE MAIN EVENT

You've organized your schedule, gathered your leaders, and prepared yourself with prayer. Get ready to challenge your teens to drop out of the popularity contest!

OPEN UP

Here's a suggestion for opening the session with prayer:

Lord, I thank you for each of the students attending this session. I ask that you would open their hearts and minds to receive the information that you would like to show them. Lord, please help our team listen to your direction, and help us be sensitive to the needs of each person attending. Lord, please help us to stand in unity with one another to fight against all these cultural norms that work against the body of Christ. We thank you in advance for the amazing work you are going to do. In Jesus' name, amen.

LEADER TIP

If any of your groups are at odd numbers instead of even, have some of your youth volunteers or leaders participate. *Groups must be in even numbers.* It's also a good idea to have supervision to help your teens get untangled when they're in a bind.

ACTIVITY: TANGLED MESS

For this opening activity, you will need to divide your teens into groups that all have an even number of teens—either six, eight, or ten teens per group. Ideally, it works well if the groups are made up of either all boys or all girls.

After your students have formed their groups, give the instructions. Be very high-energy as you start this one; they'll need it for this activity!

Goals: To show your teenagers how easily things can get all tangled up, which is often the case in friendships and relationships. (This is a point you'll be making!) Things like gossip and hooking up result in tangled friendships and relationships, and this icebreaker is a great way to get people talking about the problem. The second goal of this activity is to show your students how important it is that everyone works together. This game demonstrates everyone's value and purpose. Instead of one person seeking to be the focus, everyone has to work together in unity to successfully get untangled.

The instructions go like this:

1. Each group, form a circle!

2. Everyone put your right hand in the air.

3. Now reach over to someone else *across* your circle (NOT your neighbor on the right or left), and grab someone else's right hand.

LEADER TIP
Be sure the teens are being careful about where their hands go. Since you're in close quarters, their bodies have to be close together— and this is the main reason why we suggest all-girl and all-guy groups.

4. Raise your left hand in the air.

5. Again, reach across your circle and grab someone *else's* left hand (NOT your neighbor on the right or left OR the person you are holding with your right hand).

6. OK, now get untangled from this mess, without letting go! You must be untangled into a full circle, without any twists. If anyone in your group lets go of anyone's hand, your team will be disqualified!

Once the teens are in place and all tangled up, turn them loose with whatever fun command you wish. Whichever team gets untangled first, wins! Make the game fun by awarding prizes for the fastest group, the messiest group (the last group to get untangled), and the nicest group, or whatever other prizes you want to come up with.

YOUR VIEW
Make this activity your own with your tips, suggestions, and ideas for fun things to say or prizes to award:

Once you have a winning team and any prizes have been awarded, have your students take a seat, and move directly into the Key Discussion Points for this session. It's a good idea to continue to be in small groups for the discussion time. It may be easiest for you to keep students in their Tangled Mess groups. Or you may wish to divide your students into new small groups.

KEY DISCUSSION POINTS

★ How important was it in the Tangled Mess activity for every person in the group to work together? What made it easier to get untangled? What made it more difficult?

★ When we put others down in order to get to the top, our lives often end up looking like tangled messes. Have you seen this happen? How?

★ Have you ever forfeited real friendships in pursuit of popularity? In what ways? How did that work out?

★ We can pursue our own agenda in lots of ways, anything from dating someone you know your friend likes, to gossiping about that girl in bio, to competing out of pride on the football field—anything that we do for selfish purposes to puff ourselves up causes someone else to be put down. The Bible is really clear about this kind of behavior. For example, read what God says in Isaiah: "I will punish the world for its evil, the wicked for their sins. I will put an end to the arrogance of the haughty and will humble the pride of the ruthless" (13:11).

★ The problem with this attitude of making ourselves the best is that we forfeit the gift of unity when we're constantly seeking only our own way and how to get ahead. Have you seen ways that this has happened?

We see a tremendous example of unity in the book of Acts. Follow us for a moment to the upper room. After the disciples had an incredible encounter with the Holy Spirit, they were bonded together by the power of God in a supernatural way. While they were not perfect, they had a common goal and unified purpose: to take the message of the gospel to the ends of the earth, and that passion is still alive in our hearts today. That same kind of Spirit-infused unity is available to us now if we will only look to that common goal and purpose—Jesus Christ. The enemy knows the power of unity—that's why he is so determined to destroy it. If he can get you hung up on little things, like gossip and backbiting, then he has crippled your ability to be unified. Check out Psalm 133:1: "How good and pleasant it is when God's people live together in unity!"

Leaders, as you move into this time of discussion, we want to encourage you: don't run away from the issues! Talk about ways that unity within your group has been hurt. Talk about ways to build unity. Be very careful to apply caution and keep the students from using names or running others down.

Take this time of vulnerability to really hash things out with your teens. Call specific actions out—if you need to. If you have relationships with the teens in your group and you know of recent issues—fights between teens, gossip being spread, false accusations—you may want to set aside time with the persons involved to talk about what's going on with them and to hold them accountable for their behavior. Do so with gentleness and sensitivity; there are usually two sides to each story.

These discussions aren't to make anyone feel bad, but they're necessary to bring things into the light. Often, talking through these kinds of issues is exactly what students need. They feel they can rarely address their frustrations with each other, and adult intervention is almost always a necessity. Make sure you take the time to help the teens grow closer together—this helps with the unity factor, and in building lasting friendships.

Remember: Really be in prayer before you dive into these issues, especially for kids to have receptive hearts to receive the message, and that your attitude toward them will be Christlike.

FOR SMALL GROUPS

If you have a small group, feel free to do this activity with one group. Again, you have to make sure the group is an even number and doesn't exceed ten. Use yourself, volunteers, or other leaders to make the group an even number, if necessary.

BREAKING THE CYCLE OF MEAN

This next section is focused on bullying. Even though you may not realize it goes on in your group, in all the schools, churches, and groups we've attended, it has never *not* gone on. Whether it takes place more openly at your group meetings, or happens outside of your time with the teens (even within families), it is something that must be addressed. Here are a few quick facts (according to pacerteensagainstbullying.org, copyright © PACER Center):

★ **Each day, 160,000 kids in the U.S. stay home from school to avoid bullying.**

★ **One out of every three students reports being bullied every school year.**

★ **In America, six out of ten kids witness bullying at least once a day.**

To make sure we're all on the same page, let's take a moment to define the word *bully*—according to our team. We wanted to give a slightly broader definition than what you'd find in the dictionary. According to the GOV team, *bullying* is defined as: doing anything, whether in thought or action, that puts someone else down.

We include the "thought" piece because, as Christians, we believe that our thoughts have a great deal of influence, and that our thoughts can and will influence our behavior. Luke 6:45 says: "A good man brings good things out of the good stored up in his heart, and an evil man brings evil things out of the evil stored up in his heart. For the mouth speaks what the heart is full of." If you're constantly thinking negatively about someone, what are the chances that you'll be genuinely nice when you see that person? Pretty small, right?

The reason we take bullying so seriously is because of the long-term effects it has. Bullying damages people's identities, and it can cause them to question or doubt who they are in Christ. It can take years, sometimes decades, to heal the pain caused by bullying.

Before this next activity begins, take a good, hard look at your group of students. Privately, or with your leaders, outline the different teens and personalities in your group. Here are some common categories that we've seen.

The Bullies

What are the main ways teens bully? It may not be overt. Often, meanness is done in secret. Bullies can find ways to put their best foot forward to fool, or even influence, leaders, who may let their behavior slide because it seems harmless. Pray and seek God to reveal any hidden motives or meanness going on under the surface.

Common quotes we've heard from bullies:

★ **"I felt like as long as I made sure people were intimidated by me, I was more secure in who I was. It never occurred to me that my bad attitude would cause other people hurt or pain for a long time after they knew me."**

★ **"I had to make sure I was popular. That was the only thing I cared about. Whether or not I was hurting people totally didn't matter to me at the time. I was a really selfish person and wish someone would have called me out on my behavior."**

The Victims

What are the ways that victims handle being bullied? Do they withdraw? lash out? Teens are less likely to remain in your group if they're being bullied when they come to your church. Often, victims of bullying can fall into deep depression and in extreme cases can attempt or commit suicide.

Common quotes from victims:

★ "My family didn't have a lot of money growing up, and I couldn't afford new clothes. I was made fun of so badly for the way I dressed; I stopped going to youth group completely."

★ "The cliques in my school were the same cliques that were in my church. They were such jerks all the time, I stopped going. The leaders knew what was going on, but they never tried to intervene."

★ "When I was in high school, there were two specific people in youth group who said some really awful things to me. I was so upset because of what they said, I left church early and tried not to cry. That day I realized that the youth group was not a safe place for me to be."

The Bystanders

Many other kids do not participate in bullying, and have not been victims either. These teens need to be challenged to stand up for and protect those who are under attack. Who in your group can be influenced to stand up for other teens who are being bullied? What can you do to equip them to do this (not just in your group, but in their schools, in sports, and in other settings)?

YOUR VIEW

Ways that I've seen bullying happen among teens, or in my group, and suggestions or observations on how to deal with these problems:

It's helpful to outline your own group's issues so you know what and whom you're dealing with. You can bring the truth of Christ into the situation. Often, we as leaders will support the "in crowd" out of habit more than anything; sometimes it's simply because they're fun to be with. But you as a leader cannot show favoritism; it will only fuel the fire for the "mean" within your crew.

One of the best ways to stop bullying is by walking in the light. If you, as a youth leader, call out bullying for what it is, there's a good chance that occurrences will go down. If you think the situation is serious, pull aside the students involved and speak with them. It is critical for them to understand how damaging their negative behavior is, and that putting others down will not be tolerated.

It's also important to realize that bullies are victims themselves. Don't overlook the issues lying at the heart of their behavior. Often, bullies have learned from key influences (like their parents or siblings) how to act this way. They may have been abused, neglected, or put down in their own homes, so they naturally carry that way of dealing with issues into their other relationships. As a youth leader, you have a tremendous opportunity to help these teens develop new ways of handling anger, building friendships, and living more like Christ.

There's a different breed, however, of meanness spreading around schools, churches, and anywhere else teens hang out. Especially in the realm of cyber-bullying (using the Internet to defame your "enemies"), we're entering into a whole new stage of mean. It's essential that we give our teens strategies for dealing with negative behaviors, whether they are committing the acts them-selves or just witnessing them.

ACTIVITY: HOW WOULD YOU RESPOND?

Have your teens separate into groups of three to ten, depending on your group size, and ideally in all-guy or all-girl groups. Depending on the size and layout of your meeting space, you may want to have groups meet in different rooms. In any case, just make sure each group is far enough away from the other groups so the teens are not distracted by the conversations going on elsewhere.

Invite the group members to circle up. Leaders will read the scenarios that are provided. After each scenario, go around the circle and let each teen shout out a word that first came to mind when they heard the situation that was presented. (Note: These scenarios come from real-life events. Although they are intense and slightly graphic, we use them because they most accurately convey what teens face on a daily basis.)

After you allow the teens time to voice their feelings, move into asking the other discussion questions that follow each scenario. There are both questions for mixed groups and for guy-only or girl-only groups. Either print a copy of the discussion questions for each group or put the questions into a media presentation for all the groups to see. The time they put into this exercise may vary, but we encourage you to set aside at least twenty minutes. (Be prepared to let things go longer; it's crucial that you don't stop in the middle of making progress.)

Goals

This activity is designed to help teens do a few things:

1. Know how to respond if they are caught up in "the cycle of mean."

2. Identify if they are participating in being bullied or dishing it out.

3. See how they would react in any given circumstance.

LEADER TIP

If you have enough leaders available, have at least one appointed to each small group to keep discussions going. Don't have enough leaders? Have your leaders rotate groups, checking in frequently with all groups to make sure each is staying on track.

SCENARIOS AND QUESTIONS

SCENARIO 1: Brandon and James are two of the more popular guys in school, but they aren't guys you'd hang out with. You've seen them get wasted at a few parties, go home with way too many girls, and . . . show up at church on Sunday. They say they're Christians, but really don't act like it. You pretty much try to stay out of their way—until you find out that they've got hold of a picture of one of your friends, Kara, showing her changing after swim practice. They posted it all over the guys' locker room and are texting it to lots of people.

DISCUSSION QUESTIONS FOR ALL

1. What is your initial reaction to this story?

2. Has anything like this ever happened to you or someone you know? How was it handled? What should have been done?

3. If something like this were to happen in the future, how would you handle it?

DISCUSSION QUESTIONS FOR GUYS

1. You've probably heard it said that "boys will be boys." How do you draw the line between what is appropriate and what is not in locker-room talk?

2. Sometimes guys compete with each other about . . . lots of things—and it usually happens at the expense of someone else (like a friend or, let's say, your little sister). If you were the guy observing this happening to Kara, what would be your first reaction? How would you try to help Kara or defend her?

3. What would you do about the guys who posted the picture?

DISCUSSION QUESTIONS FOR GIRLS

1. First, it's important for you to know that if this ever happens to you, please tell an authority! Now that we've said that, how would you handle this situation if it happened to you or your friend (in addition to telling someone)?

2. If you were Kara in this story, how would you feel? What would you want to do? How would you deal with your feelings?

3. How would you feel or handle the situation if it happened to a girl you didn't like—maybe even a girl who had a bad reputation?

4. Do you think there are any preventive measures you could take to help avoid this happening to you or a "Kara" in the future?

LEADER TIP
The scenarios presented here are far more common than most adults realize. It's important to see the reality of the world today's teens live in, where many students live by a "no holds barred" approach to mobile uploads. Give your teenagers a new perspective on this issue. Ask them: "What would you do if this was your brother or sister? mom or dad? future husband or wife?"

SCENARIO 2: Last night, Mason was checking her social networking page when her friend Adam starting posting some really uncharacteristic items. Some of them were seriously nasty, even near-porn pics. The next day at school, you find out that

Adam's page had been hacked by some sicko, and now everyone is accusing Adam of being a major creeper.

DISCUSSION QUESTIONS FOR ALL

1. What is your initial reaction to this story?

2. What advice would you give to Adam?

3. Has anything like this ever happened to you or someone you know? How was it handled? What should have been done?

4. If something like this were to happen in the future, how would you handle it?

5. If we're living by the Golden Rule (treat others as you want to be treated), then we need to establish high standards about the way we treat others. If you and your friends made a contract regarding how you're going to treat people, what would be your top three rules on the list? (Have your group write them out; use a whiteboard or some other means. Committing ideas to some form of outward expression helps make them more real.)

DISCUSSION QUESTIONS FOR GUYS

1. Would you ever hack into your friend's social network, chat, or e-mail account? Do you think it's important to draw boundary lines with your friends about this kind of thing?

2. Guys often play practical jokes on each other. How do you decide when a joke goes too far?

3. How would you respond if you overheard some guys planning to do something like what was done to Adam?

DISCUSSION QUESTIONS FOR GIRLS

1. Often with girls, meanness is taken to a whole new level when it comes to social media. Has anyone ever lied to you—or about you—online, especially people you thought were your friends? Talk about that time, without using names.

2. Sometimes girls come up with subtle ways of getting back at people who have wronged them. If you had overheard girls plotting against Adam in this way, what would you have done?

3. What if you found out Adam had hurt the feelings of a girl you knew and this was her way of getting back at him? Would that change your view of what happened? Why or why not?

SCENARIO 3: You know your friend Emily has made a promise to save sex for marriage only. Some girls at church started a rumor that last weekend she went home with a guy from school named Cody, and the rumor has spread like wildfire. Now Cody is backing up these rumors with stories of his own about her. Emily is devastated by these lies, and she doesn't want to go to church or school anymore.

DISCUSSION QUESTIONS FOR ALL

1. What is your initial reaction to this story?

2. What would you do to help Emily?

3. Has anything like this ever happened to you or someone you know? How was it handled? What should have been done?

4. If something like this were to happen in the future, how would you handle it?

DISCUSSION QUESTIONS FOR GUYS

1. Guys, you may not realize that this happens to girls all the time. When girls spread these types of rumors about each other, it isn't to brag—it's to make the victimized girl look like a tramp. That kind of reputation can be brutal in girl-world, not to mention cause a great deal of harm to a girl's lifelong self-esteem. Next time you hear a trashy rumor about a girl, how do you think you will handle it?

LEADER TIP
If you have extra time, or to continue these discussions, make up your own scenarios and let the teens act them out!

2. If you're in the locker room and these kinds of stories start flying, if you don't stand up for the person (usually a girl) being attacked, you're actually aiding in hurting him or her. What do you think you could say or do to stop this from happening?

1. Ladies, we want to be very clear. This kind of behavior is totally unacceptable. We as women of God have got to stop these kinds of rumors from spreading. The next time you hear a rumor like this going around, what will you do about it?

2. If you were Emily, there are many things you could do in response: confront the girls, confront Cody, retaliate with lies of your own, etc. What are some other options you might have? What would a godly response be to such a situation?

> ### LEADER TIP
> A step you can take to help stop cyber-bullying is to appoint leaders to be in charge of monitoring the students' social networking pages. Encourage the teens to have accountability with one another about their social pages and other forms of social media—and to be accountable with an adult as well.

SCENARIO 4: Feel free to create your own scenarios with the specific issues your teens need to address. Think about events that have happened in your group in the past or even stories that have been in the headlines lately.

After discussing these scenarios, invite your students to open up about their own experiences. How have they been affected by bullying? Encourage everyone to join in the discussions, regardless of which side they may be on. Leave time at the end for prayer.

> ### LEADER TIP
> If you know a lawyer or a police officer, it might be helpful to have such a person come and talk to your teens about the kinds of legal trouble a teen can get into through cyberbul-lying and other forms of harassment. Having such a figure talk about specific, real-life conse-quences of these kinds of actions (including some of those from the scenarios you present) could help the teens take things seriously.

FOR SMALL GROUPS

It's important in a small gathering, or in small groups formed out of a larger group, to be very aware of who is in your group. If you know you have a bully in your group, try to make sure that, during discussion times, that person is separated from any of his or her victims who might also be in the session. A person who has been victimized in the past may feel intimidated about speaking up about these issues in the presence of that bully, or even just in the presence of any bully-type individual.

Keep an eye out for teens who are extraordinarily quiet during the discussion times and try to find time with them one-on-one to see how they are doing or if they want to talk about anything.

FOR WEEKEND RETREATS

Make sure every cabin/room has a printout of the discussion questions and scenarios. One option is to have groups go back to their cabins/rooms to discuss in greater privacy and in a more relaxed atmosphere. A spokesperson for each group could share their main thoughts at a later session, if needed.

FOR CAMPS

If you're doing this activity at a weekend retreat or camp, you may find that teens are much more vulnerable in discussions about popularity and bullying for two reasons: 1) They are away from their normal surroundings, and feel freer to discuss their frustrations. 2) The students are bunking with other students, and sometimes the cabins or rooms act as pressure cookers. Those who have run youth events know that a percentage of the time is spent dealing with arguments, hurt feelings, or fights. Make sure there is ample time allowed in your schedule for leaders to be able to just hang out with the teens so there are opportunities for teens to come and talk about any immediate issues.

ACTIVITY: DARTS

Note: This activity requires close adult supervision!

SUPPLIES NEEDED

★ **A target sheet mounted to a corkboard (one for every fifty or so teens)**

★ **A poster or picture of Jesus, about the same size as the target sheet, one for every target**

★ **Steel-tipped darts, at least one for every five teens (these are real darts—which is why you need the close supervision!)**

* Sticky notes (one for each student)
* One pair of scissors for every target
* Markers (various colors)
* Clear tape

You'll need to have target sheets mounted against corkboard prior to this session. We make our own target sheets out of red and white construction paper, then use clear packing tape to stick them to the corkboard. Make sure the corkboard is thick enough to withstand a dart going through it.

The secret to this activity is this: before taping the sheets to the corkboard, sandwich between the target sheet and the corkboard a large illustration of Jesus. Make sure that the picture remains hidden! It will be revealed later in the session.

LEADER TIP
Sometimes it is helpful to do a small amount of damage to the picture of Jesus prior to hiding it behind the corkboard. The reason for this is, sometimes the darts do not quite hit the illustration through the layers of paper, and the effect of seeing the picture damaged is important.

LEADER TIP
Place the targets in various locations in the meeting area before your teens arrive for this activity. Then put away the darts until you begin. You don't want any students throwing darts before it's time to do so.

Goal: This activity is designed to open teens' eyes to the powerful effect their thoughts and words can have. We want to help teens understand that even when people hurt us, we must forgive as Christ has forgiven us. Even though that can be incredibly painful at times, being set free from the burden of resentment can bring an overwhelming amount of relief. The problem is, the enemy is such a deceiver that he leads us to believe that bitterness and hatred will aid us in achieving a victory over our offenders—that revenge is the only way for us to heal. But truly, this only hurts us more. When we offer forgiveness to someone who has wronged us, we allow the light and life of Christ into our situation and healing can begin. One of the first steps to offering forgiveness is recognizing and accepting the grace that God has offered to us.

Begin this activity by gathering your teens together and sharing a story of a time when someone hurt you, and you had a difficult time forgiving. The story you share may even be something that you are working through right now. Not that everyone will have an extreme case, but it helps if the story is one that teens can easily relate to and understand how hard it was to forgive.

After you have shared the story, have volunteers pass out a sticky note to every teen. You may want to divide the teens into groups at this time, or have them already divided beforehand, matching the number of groups with the number of targets you have available.

Then you or another leader should explain that you want the teens to take some time to think of someone who has wronged them and whom they have not forgiven. Instruct the teens to write on the sticky note a word, a symbol, or a drawing that represents that person in their minds (teens should be advised to refrain from using actual names).

Then tell the group to stick their notes on the target closest to them, or the one designated for their group. After they've done that, have each group form a line in front of their target.

You'll need to wait until all the teens are lined up before the next step. When they are ready, have the leader (or leaders) who shared a story talk about the impact that event had. For example, they could

> **LEADER TIP**
> You might choose to have music playing while the teens are throwing their darts. Then, when it's time to expose the picture of Jesus, abruptly stop the music.

say something like: "You know, that person really hurt me. When he said that stuff about me, I was so embarrassed and I felt totally alone. I was angry."

Then have the person speaking write a word or drawing on a sticky note (to represent the person who wronged him or her), stick it to a target, walk to the start of the line in front of that target, and then throw a dart at the note.

The speaker could continue in this way: "Have any of you ever felt that way? Maybe your hurt happened some time ago, or maybe it is recent. Maybe it is even going on right now. But right now, if you want to, you can take a moment to admit your anger."

Then have your leaders place themselves at the head of every target line. Give each teen in line a chance to throw a dart. (Be sure only one teen in a group throws at a time.) Allow the teens to go through the line at least twice; then have them go back to their seats. Some may not want to throw a dart, and that is OK. Throwing the darts is meant to open the teens' eyes to visualize what their thoughts and words are doing.

Once everyone in all the groups is finished with the darts, collect the darts and put them away. While this is happening, you and/or other leaders bring all the targets to the front of the room.

The following are some discussion points you could share at this time.

★ **There are many times when you will be angry because of something that was done to you. But in Ephesians 4:32, Paul advised: "Be kind and compassionate to one another, forgiving each other, just as in Christ God forgave you."**

★ **Christ died on the cross for us, but he also died for the people who did these things to us. Before we lash out at anyone, it's important to stop and consider the grace that has been extended to us. Jesus, even though he was perfect and hurt no one, willingly carried all our sins and wounds and forgave us for them anyway. If he could do that for us, what do you think we, who are in no way perfect, should be able to do for others? Remember what Jesus said the King would say: "Truly I tell you, whatever you did for one of the least of these brothers and sisters of mine, you did for me" (Matthew 25:40).**

LEADER TIP
As this is an activity that can result in varying levels of emotion, it would be beneficial to have a time and even a room set aside where teens can go and speak to leaders further about their issues or have someone pray with them.

As you make this last point, you and the other leaders can cut away the target sheets, exposing the pictures of Jesus, which will likely have many holes in them now.[2]

ACTIVITY: THE MEMORIAL WALL

This activity is meant to directly follow the previous activity. However, it could also happen at a later time.

SUPPLIES NEEDED

★ **Jesus picture(s) from Darts activity**

★ **A large piece of butcher paper, plain wrapping paper, or parcel paper (enough to fill a wall)**

★ **Note cards or sheets of letter-sized paper**

★ **Markers**

★ **Clear tape**

You'll first want to separate the Jesus picture(s) from the other pieces of the targets. Then tape the Jesus poster(s) to the large piece of paper (we recommend leaving the paper on the floor during the activity, then hanging it up when you're finished). Share with the teens the following points.

KEY POINTS AND SCRIPTURES TO SHARE

★ **"Therefore, if you are offering your gift at the altar and there remember that your brother or sister has something against you, leave your gift there in front of the altar. First go and be reconciled to them; then come and offer your gift" (Matthew 5:23, 24).**

★ **Forgiveness is the first step in reconciliation. One of the ways we've found a path to forgiveness is by choosing to see the person who hurt us as a child of God—and not as an enemy.**

★ **One of the ways to defeat the anger and hurt in our own hearts is to come at the negative situation in the opposite spirit. Jesus said: "I tell you, love your**

enemies and pray for those who persecute you, that you may be children of your Father in heaven" (Matthew 5:44, 45).

★ **Remember also the words of Luke 6:27-31: "But to you who are listening I say: Love your enemies, do good to those who hate you, bless those who curse you, pray for those who mistreat you. If someone slaps you on one cheek, turn to them the other also. If someone takes your coat, do not withhold your shirt from them. Give to everyone who asks you, and if anyone takes what belongs to you, do not demand it back. Do to others as you would have them do to you." Keep reading verses 32-38 for more insight from Jesus' words.**

Place paper/cards and markers around the butcher paper on the floor, and encourage all the teens to gather around. Take a few minutes to allow each teen to write a prayer for the person(s) who hurt him or her. Encourage the teens to put the situation into God's hands. Encourage them that just because someone offers forgiveness does not mean that person condones the act that occurred. Forgiveness is our stand before God to claim that we want to let go and move forward with God, without becoming bitter or resentful or negative. As Jesus taught: "Forgive, and you will be forgiven" (Luke 6:37).

Tape all the prayers to the butcher paper and let the teens go back to their seats. Hang the paper up in a youth room, a hallway, or wherever it can be seen by the teens. We call this "The Memorial Wall." Always use it as a reminder to live together in unity, to forgive those who've hurt us, and to move forward in the freedom of Christ.

Remind your teens that the enemy is devious and has a devious goal: If he can get us divided, he can stop the message of the gospel from spreading. Though some offenses are very serious and require time and care to recover from, many of the troubles that cause division among us are minor grievances or irritations that should not be given importance, but rather be handled with grace, humility, and a sense of humor. When we work together and choose to not let stupid things come between us, we can operate at an incredible level of unity and be a real force in this world. As Paul said in Romans 8:31: "If God is for us, who can be against us?"

Before your teens leave this session, pray for and with them.

THE REVOLUTION CONTINUES

Here are a few sample text messages, Facebook updates, tweets, or e-mails you can use to connect with your group. (Shorten them as needed.) If your church's website has a youth page, use that space as well. Use the media that you know will best connect with your students.

SAMPLE MESSAGES

- How are you doing with the challenges from the last session? Have you taken these things to heart? Have you thought of the picture of Jesus?
- Where are you with the *Culture Shock* survival guide? Questions? Comments? Let me know!
- "Do unto others as you would have them do unto you."
- Who have you reached out to today?
- How's your attitude today? Does it reflect Christ?
- Try making friends with one new person today.
- Which zone are you in? Check out the *Culture Shock* survival guide and find out!
- Guard yourself against the lies of the enemy today! Remember: just because Satan was dumb enough to believe the lies, it doesn't mean you have to be!
- "Therefore encourage one another and build each other up, just as in fact you are doing." 1 Thess 5:11
- Today when someone annoys you, resist the temptation to get upset. Respond with love!

BUILDING THE BRIDGE

Use the ideas below to connect with parents to make sure they know what their kids are being told regarding the issues of bullying, forgiveness, and unity. We've also included ideas on helping the parents connect with their teens about these issues. For more resources, including weekly parent updates and key resource recommendations, visit us online at www.generationsofvirtue.org.

OVERVIEW OF THE POPULARITY CONTEST

The vicious cycle of meanness has overtaken our teenagers like a tidal wave. Gossiping, backbiting, and belittling others have become cultural norms, not exceptions.

In "The Popularity Contest," we talked with teens about how these acts only divide us, and that if we're going to reach the level of unity that Christ has called us to, we must get rid of these behaviors.

We discussed specific issues of teens harassing other teens, including cyberbullying. We talked about what to do if it happens to them or someone they know.

Last, we did an activity called Darts, which illustrated how we should not hold on to anger but instead work to forgive those who have hurt us. Then we created a Memorial Wall to remind us to forgive and move on with the power of Christ.

FIVE GREAT DISCUSSION POINTS FOR PARENTS AND TEENS

1. How did "The Popularity Contest" event cause you to evaluate the way you treat other people?

2. In the future, how will you respond when someone treats you badly? What about when you see someone treating another person poorly?

3. Where do you feel like the most bullying happens around you? Church? School? Sports?

4. Why do you feel that things such as gossiping, bullying, and meanness are problems? What is so bad about them?

5. What are some things you learned during this event that we could use to create more unity in our home?

CONNECT: AN ACTIVITY FOR PARENTS AND TEENS

To keep alive what the teens learned in "The Popularity Contest," create a Code of Conduct for your home. Say something like: "Just like we did for the media guidelines, let's come up with ideas that specifically outline how we treat both those in our family and those in the world around us." This is a great way to set clear expectations for teens on what behavior is acceptable and what is not. Here's an example:

OUR FAMILY'S CODE OF CONDUCT

1. We will not gossip, belittle, or backbite one another. If we have a problem, we will talk it out when we are not angry. When we *do* get angry, we will walk away and then return when we are able to discuss the issue without yelling or saying something that we will regret.

2. We will not engage in conversations where people are being made fun of or talked about behind their backs.

3. If someone is being cyberbullied, we commit to going and telling an authority figure who can get involved.

4. When someone hurts us, we commit to forgive that person, no matter how difficult it is. We choose to love one another as Christ has loved us.

5. In our words, thoughts, and actions, we commit to honoring and loving one another. If we wouldn't want it said or done to us, then we won't say or do it to others.

Include whatever you can come up with for helping your teen and family break the cycle of mean! After you create your Code of Conduct, print it out and place it at different spots in your house and go over it together on occasion. Have it handy when something comes up that goes against the Code.

PLUG IN

Youth leaders should be sure to e-mail parents to communicate with them about what their teens have been discussing and learning. Feel free to send them the Overview of the session and the Five Great Discussion Points. Introduce them to the idea of the Connect activity as well. Include your contact information so parents can reach you if they have questions. For tons of resource help and parenting tips, parents can check out www.generationsofvirtue.org. Encourage them also to discuss the *Culture Shock* survival guide with their teens to inspire even more conversations.

Make use of Facebook updates, Twitter messages, texts, and e-mail to send messages of encouragement and connection to the parents. If they don't use any of these forms of communication, find out what works best for them (a phone call, brief meetings). Just keep the communication lines open!

- Did you know that bullying affects at least one in three teens? Is your teen one of them? Find out!
- Six out of every ten teens witness bullying every day. How does it affect your teen?
- Parents, today your teenagers committed to stop gossiping about each other! Will you make the same commitment?
- This event taught us so much about unity! Learning about Psalm 133:1 was awesome!
- Ask your teen about the challenges in the *Culture Shock* survival guide. Has he or she started a clean campaign yet?
- Is your teen a bully, a victim, or a bystander? Ask your teen and find out more.
- Pray with your teen tonight about anything that came up today, especially about his or her friends.
- Is your teen keeping your family's Code of Conduct? In what areas is he or she struggling?

FEARLESS PURITY

C hrist has given us an incredible promise when it comes to purity: "Blessed are the pure in heart, for they will see God" (Matthew 5:8). Often, however, our own tainted views of love and sex have caused some of us, as leaders, to shy away from really focusing on the message of purity. Though we all want our teens to save sex for marriage, we have to be thoughtful in our approach to these issues concerning their private lives. If our students, with all the pressures they face every single day, are going to hold on to purity and live with integrity, they are going to need a serious road map.

We believe that when you can see purity from God's awesome perspective, it becomes really exciting to open up about your life and experiences with your teens. Don't be afraid to share what is on your heart. It will make you much more vulnerable with them, and the teens in our audiences have always responded with appreciation for our personal stories and testimonies. So please keep in mind while preparing for this event that being transparent and honest can make your message come alive.

Teens value honesty and authenticity! Being sincere with them can build a bridge of trust between you that you may have thought impossible.

THE LEADER'S CHALLENGE

This message is really only effective if *you, as leaders, are practicing what you preach*. If you're cautioning your teens against entertaining sexual thoughts, masturbating, watching porn, and pushing physical boundaries, yet your private life is harboring seduction and lust—the message that you preach will not be effective. We want to challenge you to a higher level of purity in your personal life so that the Spirit of God can flow through you in a greater and more powerful way.

LEADER TIP
During your thirty-day challenge, we encourage you to keep a journal. You never know when you'll be able to use what you've learned to help your teens break through their struggles.

If you want to see true breakthroughs within your group—like addictions broken and teens who are in passionate pursuit of their first love (Revelation 2:4)—then it has to start with you. You, as the authority, have to be the one to draw the line in the sand and say, "Enough is enough." God told Joshua to stand before all Israel and say, "Sanctify yourselves for tomorrow, because thus says the LORD God of Israel: '*There is* an accursed thing in your midst, O Israel; you cannot stand before your enemies until you take away the accursed thing from among you'" (Joshua 7:13, *NKJV*). Just like Joshua, we're not able to fight against the enemy of our souls if we're harboring things that are in direct rebellion against the Spirit of God.

We wrote this thirty-day challenge for you to begin "Fearless Purity." We know it can be tough to break free from old patterns, but we fully believe that the blood of Christ absolutely gives us the power to do it. The study is a full thirty days for a reason—some experts believe that it takes twenty-one days for an activity to become a habit, so we want to go a step further and do this for a whole month (just for good measure)!

Here is your challenge: First, pray. Ask God what areas he wants you to change (some might be obvious, others a little harder to see). Find an accountability partner—preferably someone older and wiser. And remember: same sex is a must. (If you're married and are not being totally open with your spouse, however—NOW would be the time to do so.) Next, go to www.generationsof virtue.org/cultureshock/leaderschallenge.html for your Daily Purity Challenge.

Before you dive into this session, besides doing the Challenge, take some time to:

★ **READ—Read through the session, of course, but also spend time in the Scriptures suggested throughout. The main passages are: Proverbs 4:23; 12:14; Song of Solomon 2:7; Matthew 5:8; 18:20; Titus 2:7, 8; James 4:7. Read the surrounding verses or chapters of these passages so you are aware of the context.**

* **WATCH**—In the time leading up to your session or event, watch out for specific examples of messages about sex in television shows, advertising, movies, video games, magazines, online content, and other media aimed at teens. Having these examples fresh in your mind may be helpful as you lead your group.

* **PRAY**—Ask God for wisdom for yourself and your fellow leaders. Pray for compassion and openness as you lead discussions with your teens. Pray for specific girls and guys you know who need to hear this message.

BREAKING IT DOWN

For camps and weekend retreats, it is possible to complete this event in one day. For large groups and small groups, "Fearless Purity" can be extended to fill two or three weeks instead of just one sitting. Here are some different breakdown options:

1. Use this as a longer event by breaking it into three sessions:

* **Session One: Broken Hearts activity and Honesty 101 panel.**

* **Session Two: Go over the panel discussions from the previous session and do the Intentional Purity activity.**

* **Session Three: Share personal testimonies and complete the Pledge of Honor ceremony. Allow time at the end of the session for prayer with individual teens who have been moved by the session or need encouragement.**

2. Break it into two sessions:

* **Session One: Broken Hearts activity and Honesty 101 panel. End the session with the Intentional Purity activity.**

* **Session Two: Share personal testimonies and complete the**

Pledge of Honor ceremony. Allow time at the end of the session for prayer with individual teens who have been moved by the session or need encouragement.

3. Use this as a one-session event, building in enough time for all the aforementioned activities, sharing of testimonies, and prayer.

No matter how you break it down, be sure to encourage your teens to dive deep into their *Culture Shock* survival guides before and after the sessions.

THE MAIN EVENT

O nce you've decided how to organize your sessions, prepared yourself and your team, gathered your teens, and given it all over to God, you're ready to dig deep into a discussion on purity!

SEND THIS MESSAGE

Make this loud and clear to your students from the start:

★ **It *is* possible to be pure in heart, mind, and body.**

★ **Remember that purity is war, where battles can be fought and won. As you are fighting this battle, never align yourself with the enemy. We have to learn what our personal enemies are so that we can abolish them from our lives. Remember James 4:7: "Submit yourselves, then, to God. Resist the devil, and he will flee from you."**

OPEN UP

Here's a suggestion for opening the session with prayer:

God, thank you for everyone present. We ask that you would make clear to us all the things we're about to learn about living pure lives for you. Please give us wisdom about what to change so that we can honor you with our hearts, minds, and bodies. Amen.

ACTIVITY: BROKEN HEARTS

For this activity you'll need two leaders to play emcees, and two leaders or student volunteers to play the main boy and girl roles. You'll also need a red paper heart for every person in a role in the skit. And be sure to set aside two whole red paper hearts to show at the end.

LEADER TIP

Take a minute to handpick people for the main roles in this activity. Our experience has been that the funnier, more dramatic people help make this activity really memorable!

Goal: The point of this activity is to illustrate that each temporary relationship or crush you give your heart to, opening yourself up to physical and emotional intimacy, does some damage to your heart when those bonds get broken, making it difficult for you to trust and to give your heart fully and uncon-ditionally when the time comes to enter into a permanent relationship.

Give every person in a role a red paper heart. You can follow our sample script below or, better yet, make up your own! Besides the players of the main roles, think about which audience participants you will pick as well. We've found it best if leaders who are favorites among the teens play active roles in the skit. The teens will tend to pay more attention if they can connect with the leaders chosen.

The Story

(CAYDEN and OLIVIA stand in the stage area, holding their paper hearts. EMCEE 1 and 2 stand off to one side of the stage.)

EMCEE 1: Meet Cayden and Olivia. Let's pretend that they are . . . both twelve years old. Everyone say: "Hey, Cayden and Olivia!"

(Waits for crowd to respond.)

EMCEE 1 OR 2: They meet for the first time at youth group, and love is in the air!

EMCEE 1: So Cayden finally gets the courage to ask Olivia out, and she says YES! Don't they look cute together?

(CAYDEN and OLIVIA trade hearts.)

EMCEE 1 OR 2: This relationship was going so well—it had lasted a whole *two weeks*! Cayden and Olivia had already kissed, but hadn't gone any further. Just a short while later, Olivia starts getting irritated with Cayden, and now she has her eye on someone else. She marches up to Cayden during football practice and shouts, "Cayden, I'm done! You can just forget it!" They break up.

(They rip each other's hearts in half, then give the pieces back. OLIVIA stomps offstage. EMCEE 1 waits a moment for CAYDEN to show reaction. Then, while talking, selects a girl from the crowd and leads him over to her.)

EMCEE 1: Cayden is so heartbroken over Olivia! But then at fifteen he meets this other girl—Jane—in the library. It's definitely love! He asks her out, and she says YES!

(CAYDEN and JANE exchange hearts [heart pieces, for CAYDEN] and look at each other with adoration.)

This relationship lasts a long time—*three whole months*! Now, they are definitely spending way too much time together—without clothing. Then one day, out of the blue, Cayden texts Jane and says, "You're too clingy. I'm done." They break up!

(CAYDEN and JANE rip each other's hearts or heart pieces, give the pieces back, and walk offstage. OLIVIA walks onstage alone. While this is happening, EMCEE 1 picks a random boy from the crowd and leads him to wait offstage.)

EMCEE 2: After she broke up with Cayden, Olivia had several crushes (OLIVIA could crush her heart pieces a few times here), and eventually dated a guy for a whole *six months*!

(EMCEE 1 brings random guy onstage [who does NOT have a heart] and has him take OLIVIA's heart pieces and walk hand-in-hand with her for a few steps.)

But soon after their six-month anniversary, he broke up with her, breaking her heart. (Random guy casually tears heart and gives pieces back to OLIVIA, then sits back down in the audience.) So she waited a while to start dating again.

Now she's seventeen, and one day while hanging out with her friends at a coffee shop, she strikes up a conversation with this cute guy! (EMCEE 1 walks OLIVIA over to a new guy from the audience and gives him a heart to hold.) His name is Jared—and she is *totally* in love! (OLIVIA pushes her heart pieces onto JARED. He gives her his heart, more slowly.)

Without much thought, Olivia gives Jared her heart—and a LOT more, for that matter. Jared and Olivia stay together for *a year*, but then he decides to go out of state for college. He waves good-bye to Olivia—and she never sees him again.

(OLIVIA and JARED act out this scene. JARED tears her heart, gives the pieces back, and goes back to sit with the audience. OLIVIA tears JARED's heart and gives it back.)

Olivia is tired of getting hurt. She decides to stop dating until she is older.

EMCEE 1: Cayden is still lookin' for love at age twenty—he still hasn't found Miss Right! While overseas teaching English to foreigners, he meets *this* beautiful young lady. (EMCEE 2 walks CAYDEN over to a new girl from audience. EMCEE 2 gives ANNA a heart to hold.)

Since Cayden and Anna are both new to this foreign land, things progress pretty quickly with the two of them. (They exchange hearts [and pieces].) They move in together, and at first things seem OK. But after *two years* they realize it isn't going to work out, and they break up. (They tear each other's hearts and return the pieces. ANNA sits back down.)

EMCEE 2: At twenty-five years old, Cayden reluctantly moves back to his hometown, discouraged and disappointed that he hasn't found his true love. In the meantime, Olivia also decides to move back to her hometown to help take care of her elderly grand-parents. They both begin going to church again, and have incredible encounters with Christ. After months of attending the same church without realizing it, Olivia and Cayden lock eyes for the first time since they were twelve years old—and sparks fly! They get to know one another all over again, and through lots of prayer, Cayden and Olivia decide to get married!

(CAYDEN and OLIVIA act out the aforementioned scenario. Then they stand as if at an altar, getting married. EMCEE 1 acts as the minister.)

EMCEE 1 (ACTING AS MINISTER): Jesus said, "For this reason a man will leave his father and mother and be united to his wife, and the two will become one flesh. . . .

Therefore what God has joined together, let no one separate." I now pronounce you man and wife. Join your hearts.

(CAYDEN and OLIVIA attempt to put their confetti-like pieces of hearts together as one. As the pieces fall to the ground, both of them look dismayed/act upset. EMCEE 1 shakes head in disapproval. Then EMCEE 2 walks onstage and stands in between CAYDEN and OLIVIA, holding two whole hearts.)

EMCEE 2: Now guys, wouldn't it have been *so* much better if you had just waited for the one that God had for you? God wants to save you from heartbreak and pain, and all this trouble now. I'm not saying God can't mend a broken heart. He absolutely can. But it isn't as easy as the world makes it out to be; it can take years to heal a broken heart. And even when those hearts are restored, the consequences of those broken relationships are still out there. That's why it's so important to guard your heart.

(EMCEE 1 could have each of the former boyfriends/girlfriends file across the stage, picking up a piece of heart and taking it with him/her. They walk offstage and sit back down. After this, EMCEE takes up position as minister again. EMCEE 2 gives CAYDEN and OLIVIA each a new whole heart.)

EMCEE 1: What God joins together now, let no one separate. I now pronounce you man and wife. You may join your hearts. (CAYDEN and OLIVIA put their two hearts together as one.)

KEY DISCUSSION POINTS

★ **In Song of Solomon 2:7, the writer says "not to awaken love until the time is right" (NLT). Now, why on earth would we choose to "not awaken love"? Everything around us is screaming, "HELLO! You HAVE to date! You HAVE to mess around! You HAVE to experience all that sex and relationships have to offer!" We have to realize what we're actually doing when we forfeit our hearts to relationships outside of marriage.**

★ **Proverbs 4:23 says to "Guard your heart above all else, for it determines the course of your life" (NLT). That is pretty intense. Your heart—whether whole or in pieces—will determine how your life turns out. That is why it's so critical that we guard who affects our hearts and who we allow into them. If we let any guy or girl that we're attracted to have control in our hearts, it's like giving them the keys and saying, "Here—you can determine the direction my life goes."**

★ **This isn't just about physical relationships! Emotional intimacy at the wrong time can do just as much harm as physical intimacy. They both can impact us the same way. In either instance, we end up forming a bond that will eventually be broken.**

★ **When we get into and out of relationships that God did not design, we are letting people, not God, author our life. And that is a scary place to be.**

Leaders, do you have a relevant story? You don't need to tell all the details, but being vulnerable and sharing your past mistakes and successes in relationships can make this segment even more powerful.

FOR SMALL GROUPS

This activity is a great icebreaker! Since it's funny and lighthearted, it loosens the teens up while giving you a platform for diving into the more serious issues. If you don't have enough leaders or teens in your group to fill all the roles in the activity, have people do dual roles or adjust the script as necessary.

FOR WEEKEND RETREATS

We encourage you to do this activity earlier in the day, then let the teens process it until a later session. This gives them time to prepare for what they're going to hear. One thing we've found is that if teens know all day that you are going to talk about sexual purity later, they come more prepared to listen.

FOR CAMPS

See note above for weekend retreats. You could opt to do the skit earlier in the day, then have cabin leaders go over the discussion points with the teens in their cabins in the evening.

ACTIVITY: HONESTY 101

This next section is designed to help your group determine specific standards regarding purity. Use markers and a whiteboard—or a similar writing surface—to write out standards for your group. Preselect a mixed panel of trusted adult leaders, parents, youth leaders, and teens to participate in discussions from the stage. You will be asking your panel the questions from the Key Discussion Points. Let each panel member have a chance to respond. As each question is explored, summarize the main points on the board. As God told Habakkuk in 2:2 (*NLT*), "Write my answer plainly on tablets, so that a runner can carry the correct message to others."

LEADER TIP

Feel free to have your teens create their own questions for the panel to answer during this section. Just make sure to read and filter through the questions first! (You never know what kinds of questions you'll get!) You could even have the students text their questions to you! Feel free to tweak this format according to your media capabilities, group size, and volunteer staff.

KEY PANEL DISCUSSION POINTS

Each of these main questions is followed by several more specific questions to enhance the conversation.

1. There are three ways to bond to another person; when done in the wrong season of life, they can end with us forfeiting our hearts. These ways are: physically, emotionally, and spiritually. Let's begin with the first and most obvious: physical. Questions for the panel:

A. At what point do you become physically bonded to someone? Is it through kissing? hand holding? hugging? intercourse? (Allow your panel to provide various answers.)

B. Share this excerpt from *The Female Brain*, by Louann Brizendine, a neuropsychiatrist at the University of California: "From an experiment on hugging, we also know that oxytocin is naturally released in the brain after a twenty-second hug from a partner—sealing the bond between the huggers and triggering the brain's trust circuits. So don't let a guy hug you unless you plan to trust him."[3] Ask the panel: If we can be bonded to someone during a brief hug, where do you think the lines should be drawn in your relationships?

C. How do you avoid becoming physically bonded to someone? Allow the panel to answer. The GOV team suggests side hugs instead of full frontal hugs with people to whom you are attracted, or even withholding all physical affection in such cases. We definitely encourage teens not to kiss. We know it's a tall order—but if teenagers can

hold to this high standard, it is so much less likely that they will fall into sexual temptation. Starting something sexually and then stopping is difficult at any age, and harder still for hormone-driven teenagers. Also, based on research compiled by Drs. Joe McIlhaney and Freda McKissic Bush in *Hooked: New Science on How Casual Sex Is Affecting Our Children*, we know that kissing bonds us physically to the person we're locking lips with, and that engaging repeatedly in temporary physical bonds creates a pattern that interferes with the development of healthy long-term relational bonds.[4] As teenagers, there is no reason to bond in this way to anyone, because you're just not ready for a marriage relationship. It is critical that your ability to physically bond with your future husband or wife is left entirely intact for marriage. We all know—or any married person will tell you—how much work marriage takes!

D. Why do we want to avoid physically bonding to someone with whom we *aren't* in a long-term relationship (as opposed to family members, close same-sex friends, etc.)?

2. How and why should we guard against bonding *emotionally* to the opposite sex? We're talking about an unhealthy emotional bond, such as happens in a romantic relationship in which one or both persons aren't ready.

A. How do two people bond emotionally? What happens for this to occur?

B. Is it possible to get your heart broken by someone to whom you are only emotionally attached? Can you get your heart broken by someone you aren't even dating?

C. What methods can we use to distance ourselves and guard our hearts against premature emotional attachments? Some suggested answers include: avoid talking about deep or intimate subjects, making yourself emotionally vulnerable, or sharing personal secrets with someone who could be a romantic interest.

From the GOV team:

This is where one of the critical differences between guys and girls comes into play. We believe guys and girls can be good friends. However, years of working with teenagers has shown us that when a guy says "good friends" and a girl says "good friends," they often mean two very different things!

When a guy has declared that a girl is a friend, he is usually not going to fall in love with her or think of her as a date. That doesn't mean he won't ever be attracted to her physically—sex is often not far from the teenage guy's mind—but it generally means he has set her apart from another category of girls he would like to be romantically connected with.

When a girl has a close guy friend, she is usually very connected to him emotionally, and rather than ruling him out as a date, she may fall in and out of love with him multiple times. It's important to recognize and understand these differences so you can address them with your teens.

3. What about spiritual bonding? As we explore whether it is good to do (or not), what kinds of things do you think would make you spiritually bonded to someone?

A. Do you think it's a good idea to pray one-on-one with the opposite sex? Why or why not?

B. Since our deepest relationship is meant to be with God, when we encounter him— through prayer, worship, or in other ways— we become bonded to those we experience the encounter with. Are there ways you've seen this happen? Talk about those times.

C. How and why do you think you should avoid spiritually bonding to people to whom you are romantically attracted? Suggested answers: Pray and discuss spiritual issues in groups, not one-on-one with the opposite sex; have accountability partners, but make sure guys are with guys and girls are with girls. Guys and girls should especially not be sharing details of sexual sins with members of the opposite sex.

YOUR VIEW

List other discussion questions that you'd like your expert panel to address:

At this point, your group may have come up with some interesting answers for these questions! Now is a great time for you, as the leader, to clearly outline godly standards. These standards are good things to make as "house rules" for your youth group. Write out your expectations, along with scriptural support, when possible. For example:

★ **We pray in groups. "For where two or three gather in my name, there am I with them" (Matthew 18:20).**

★ **We keep our hands to ourselves (yep, just like in preschool). "From the fruit of their lips people are filled with good things, and the work of their hands brings them reward" (Proverbs 12:14).**

★ **Accountability partners must be of the same gender. "In everything set them an example by doing what is good. In your teaching show integrity, seriousness and soundness of speech that cannot be condemned, so that those who oppose you may be ashamed because they have nothing bad to say about us" (Titus 2:7, 8).**

MORE KEY DISCUSSION POINTS

After you've gone over your rules, go over the second part of Song of Solomon 2:7 (*NLT*), where it says "until the time is right." How do we know when the right time is? We at GOV believe that the right time involves several different things being in the right place, including:

★ **Being at an age at which you can mentally, spiritually, emotionally, financially, and physically care for your spouse.**

★ **Being spiritually grounded in the Lord, and being able to know and understand his will for your life.**

★ **Already pursuing God with all your heart, mind, soul, and strength.**

★ **Being able to raise a family (yes, we mean you need to be old enough to care for a child).**

★ **Being mature enough to make healthy, stable decisions.**

Chances are huge that when you're in middle school or high school, this isn't where you are in life.

Instead, now is the time to use your energy (emotional, physical, spiritual) to develop who you are in Christ and to become wholly bonded to him. The most incredible love stories on this earth take place when a person allows God to be at the very center. Remember: "God is love" (1 John 4:16). He is our soul's deepest connection. We can't have an incredible love story without the creator of love.

Note: Be sure to copy the standards that you came up with and communicate them to the parents of your teenagers. Make certain you're able to articulate what you came up with and why. The parents will be your biggest advocates in implementing these standards on a day-to-day basis with your students. It's critical that parents and teenagers are on the same page with these standards.

FOR SMALL GROUPS

You know your teens best. If you know of specific issues regarding purity within your small group, use this opportunity to gently and sensitively address them through carefully thought-out panel questions.

FOR WEEKEND RETREATS

Use this opportunity to involve your adult and youth leaders in a session together. If parents are available, you also can plan to have the session at a time when they can be involved in the panel discussion or simply be onlookers.

FOR CAMPS

Due to location/timing, it may be more difficult to include other leaders and parents in the panel activity in the camp setting. Consider recording the panel's discussion (taking care to keep the teens who are asking questions anonymous) so that you can share it with other leaders or with parents when you return from camp.

ACTIVITY: INTENTIONAL PURITY

This next activity can be done as a whole group. We suggest having volunteer leaders available to help the teens develop ideas, if they need assistance.

SUPPLIES NEEDED

★ **Three large signs taped in various areas of the room with these titles: Purity of Heart, Purity of Mind, and Purity of Body**

★ **At least three note cards for each teen**

★ **Pens, pencils, or markers**

If teens are going to be pure, it will take intentional effort. Now is the time to brainstorm ideas on how your students are going to walk pure in their daily lives.

Pass out three note cards for each teen present. Each note card is for three different topics: Purity of Heart, Purity of Mind, and Purity of Body. Give your students five to ten minutes to brainstorm at least one practical way to stay pure for each topic; then have them tape their cards under the correlating signs. Look at the examples that follow.

★ **"Memorizing one Scripture a week and quoting it when I get tempted" would go under Purity of Mind**

★ **"Don't hang out alone one-on-one with the opposite sex" would go under Purity of Body**

After your students are finished, go over some of the ideas that they came up with, and add any additional ideas that you as the leader feel need to be included. Later, one of your leaders can use these ideas to create a collage as a reminder for your teens to live pure every day.

Also, it would be awesome to use the ideas as social networking posts, text messages, or other updates!

YOUR VIEW

List the ideas you have for Purity of Heart, Purity of Mind, and Purity of Body:

FOR SMALL GROUPS

Keep the momentum going and move directly into the next session.

FOR WEEKEND RETREATS

See the suggestion below for camps. When you've finished this activity, we recommend taking a break before the next session. The testimony portion is an excellent one to do in the evening.

FOR CAMPS

For a fun twist on this activity, you can turn it into a competitive game. Divide your students into groups and see which team can come up with the most ideas in the given time. You also can make the sections difficult to get to, like on a stage or down the hall, so the teens have to run to tape their ideas.

PERSONAL TESTIMONIES

One of the most important elements of this session is the diversity of testimonies. But a huge mistake we sometimes see in youth conferences, at events, in small groups, and in other settings is when the only stories heard are those of failure. We encourage people to share positive stories, of those who were able to maintain a godly focus in their young lives. Teens need to be able to see that they *can* do this! They can hold on to purity and live with integrity.

Will it be difficult? Of course it will! Will it be worth it? Absolutely. Even if you or your teens have made some serious mistakes about purity, there's a huge opportunity to start over and make things new. Remember, in Revelation 21:5, God said: "I am making everything new!" It's *never* too late to start living a life of purity.

However, it is important to share both sides of this reality. And those sharing testimonies that include more struggles should be encouraged to also include the positive side, telling what God has brought them through and how they have changed or are learning to change their actions to lead a different life.

Pray very carefully about those you ask to share their testimonies! You absolutely want to make sure they are people who have sincerely changed their lifestyles and have been walking this out for a minimum of one year. It would also be good for the leaders who are sharing their stories to have completed the thirty-day Daily Purity Challenge for leaders (www.generations ofvirtue.org/cultureshock/leaderschallenge.html).

LEADER TIP

Get your leadership team together and share your testimonies well before you hold this event so you can avoid surprises, but also so you can encourage each other and pray for each other. It's also helpful to know who might have the most relevant experience to speak to a particular teen who needs counsel. Share the good and the bad—it's great to see what God has done and is doing in each other's lives.

On the next few pages are some sample testimonies from two of our team members—these have been shared with thousands of teens and groups of twenty-somethings. You may use these as encouragement for your fellow leaders or for your teens.

Tim: The Poster Christian

I grew up in the "perfect" Christian home. My parents loved God and so did I. We went to church every Sunday and I was always really popular with everyone in my age group. Life was all well and happy until my parents decided to move to a different state.

Once we moved, I felt alone, with no friends to talk to for a long time. I was building relationships from scratch, and I hated it; I just wanted a real friend. I turned to the computer for friendship.

I pretended that everything was OK, hiding my emotions because "real men don't cry"—or so I thought. But one day after I had spent hours playing games on the computer, my mom told me to stop and asked me, "Tim, why are you on that computer so much?" I couldn't hold it back anymore. I started weeping and finally had the courage to say, "It feels like someone is in the computer playing games with me. I'm so lonely. It is the only thing that helps."

A few months later I went to a local youth group and listened to everyone as they gave their testimonies and shared about how they were into drugs, sex, alcohol, pornography—I mean seriously, all kinds of stuff. But all the stories ended with God delivering them, and now their relationship with God is way better than it was before. That night I asked myself, *Is it really necessary to go through all that stuff to have a better relationship with God?* It sounded like a stupid question at the time, but because I was willing to question my motives for getting into trouble, it saved me from a world of hurt, pain, and regret.

A few years later, after struggling with *Should I dive into sin or not?* I realized I could fully dive into God, headfirst.

> I made a choice as a Christian to live to a higher standard and calling, one that was honoring both to God and to my future wife.

In order to symbolize my commitment to purity, at age sixteen, I asked my pastor to knight me. You know, like real "knights of the round table" stuff. So one afternoon, my pastor anointed me with oil and knighted me with a heavy, metal sword and a Bible, while I knelt in front of an old, wooden cross. That day meant the world to me. It truly changed my life forever.

Now I am proudly pursuing God with everything I am. I've met politicians, Christian leaders, heads of militaries, and even a prince and princess! God has taken me all over the world because I chose to say yes to him rather than to the world. What an amazing journey this has been.

Kelsey: The Jaw–Dropper

My dad was a pastor. Other than a few issues here and there, I grew up in a relatively healthy environment. When I was young, I had such a deep love for God. I hungered for more of Jesus, read my Bible, and prayed almost constantly.

Then I hit about thirteen years old.

I loved God, but I also loved . . . boys. And better yet, the feelings were mutual! I had great spiritual mentors in my life, but the less time I spent with them and the more time I spent with friends from school, the less interested in God I became.

I got asked out by one of the most popular guys in school, and that led me downhill—fast. We started messing around physically, and I became really attached. When he moved away to college, we decided to break up. After that I sought love and attention from any guy I could find. Sex, drinking, and parties became my highest priorities, and sadly, my once-strong commitment to Jesus Christ fell by the wayside.

Finally, at nineteen, things came to a serious halt. On my way to meet up with my boyfriend I was seeing secretly, I got into a terrible car wreck that almost took my life. I remember coming home from the hospital, in tremendous pain from my broken bones and inner turmoil. "God," I cried. "What is going on?"

Right then, with the afternoon sun coming in through the window, I heard God speak to me so clearly. *Kelsey—your life is like that car. Going nowhere and in pieces. Because of my mercy, I'm giving you another chance. Give me your heart.* Sobbing, I began to pray. *But God . . . my heart . . . it's in one million pieces. I have nothing to give you.* God, in his loving-kindness, brought peace to my inner turmoil and spoke again: *Kelsey, I am the great physician. I can do what you cannot do. I can put your heart back together. I can protect it, and it will be like new.*

> **My life was never the same after that. God had given me the grace to know and understand his tremendous love for me. I asked him for strength to love him and serve him—and he answered me exceedingly, abundantly beyond anything I could have ever asked for. I immediately changed my lifestyle of wild parties and sexual sin. I stopped drinking. I stopped having sex. I stopped dating. I stopped partying. I even changed the way I dressed. And I left all my crazy friends. That's right. I completely stopped talking to them and hanging out with them. I knew that they had the power to pull me down into that lifestyle again. I changed my e-mail addresses and my phone numbers. And I made a promise to God that day. I promised him that I wouldn't kiss another man until my wedding day. I had to set up roadblocks to prevent me from ever returning to that lifestyle of darkness and sin.**

I began to reflect on my life and ask where I'd gone wrong. I knew deep in my heart that it didn't happen overnight! I realized that it had started by crossing just one line: "We will totally stop at kissing." And then that line got crossed, and the next time I went further than before. Later, I had promised myself, "If I do get pregnant, we would keep the baby. Abortion is out of the question."

Over time, things had gone completely out of control. Within months I had found myself sitting in an abortion clinic, scared out of my mind, knowing that if I was pregnant, I was willing to sacrifice my child to cover up my foolish actions. That experience taught me truly how far I was willing to go, and how seriously drenched in sin my life was. There were no limits at that point. All lines had been crossed. These were all things I'd sworn I'd never do. So how did it all come about? By crossing that first line.

After completely leaving that lifestyle behind, I committed to never crossing another line. That sounds extreme, and it is! It took serious accountability and surrounding myself with supportive friends. Seven years, four-and-a-half months later, I married the guy of my dreams. Our first kiss was indeed on our wedding day! It was beautiful, and worth every second of waiting. My life is a testament of what God can do, in spite of myself! He can turn anything around, but you have to seriously commit to letting him fix you up. It's painful, happy, excruciating, and exhilarating—and worth every second!

Allow time for testimonials from students you have spoken with before the session. Make sure that what they share will be appropriate, beneficial, and sincere.

Tell your teens to check out testimonies from the GOV team and others in *Culture Shock: A Survival Guide for Teens* and online at www.generationsof virtue.org.

KEY DISCUSSION POINTS

★ **God cares even more than you do about your love life! The enemy will tell you that God doesn't care who you date, who you marry, or when—recognize that as a lie!**

★ **Take your love life very seriously—start praying for your relationships! Pray every day! Ask God to take control of this area of your life.**

YOUR VIEW

More key points to share with your group:

ACTIVITY: PLEDGE OF HONOR

After the leaders share their testimonies, we encourage you to do a Pledge of Honor with your teens. This idea runs far beyond just a physical commitment to purity. This pledge is designed to help teens live a lifestyle of purity of heart, mind, and body, and to honor God with all their hearts, minds, and strength. A sample of our pledge can be found and downloaded at www.generationsofvirtue.org. Or write your own pledge, one that will fit your students.

While your students are seated, explain the Pledge of Honor, that it is a commitment before God and these witnesses that you are aiming to lead a life that is fully honoring to our Lord Jesus Christ. Say something like: "Commitments are serious, and they are meant to be kept. Making this commitment will mark the day that you begin fighting for your purity and your future—so don't be surprised when you encounter resistance! The enemy of our souls would absolutely love to knock you off track as soon as you're motivated to commit to purity, but don't give up! Keep fighting! Keep pressing onward for your purity. Imagine when you stand before Christ—what an incredible moment it will be when you are able to tell him that you fought and won the battle for your purity."

Ask your students to raise their hands if they want to fill out the pledge that you've printed for your group. *Don't assume they want to.* If they are filling it out, it must be their choice, not something forced on them.

While your youth leaders pass out the pledges, read the pledge aloud for the whole group. After you've read it, let the teens who are ready to do so sign their pledges. After they do, pray for them to seal the commitment they've made.

CLOSING PRAYER

God, thank you for every person here. Our prayer to you is that you be very real to all of us, and that we would be seeking you first in our lives. Clean us, God, of all the impurities that would try to ruin the awesome lives you have in store for us. Amen.

> ## LEADER TIP
> We would encourage you to close this session with an opportunity for teens to come forward for prayer. Since most teens are involved in some kind of high-risk sexual behavior, it is safe to assume that at least some of the students in your group are currently sexually active. This session often opens up their perspective on the dangers of sex and the benefits of waiting, and they are often looking for prayer and encouragement when it is finished.

> ## LEADER TIP
> Consider inviting parents to the Pledge of Honor ceremony. Regardless of the setting in which you are using "Fearless Purity," we believe the presence of parents has tremendous impact and value for teens. For the teens without parents in attendance, be sure to have leaders available to stand in the gap.

THE REVOLUTION CONTINUES

It's imperative that you follow up with your teens on a regular basis about the topics discussed in this session. Think about this: the average teen watches TV and media for more than seven hours a day, every day. They're constantly bombarded with sexual influences from the media and peers; these messages rarely, if ever, have their best interest in mind. Especially remember this: Statistically, across all age groups, teens who saw the most sex on TV were twice as likely to initiate intercourse within the next year as were those who saw the least amount of sexual content.[5]

Another thing to keep in mind is the music they're listening to, because it also has a huge effect. In 2009, *Science Daily* posted an article that confirmed, "In an article published in the April 2009 issue of the *American Journal of Preventive Medicine*, researchers found that teenagers who preferred popular songs with degrading sexual references *were more likely to engage in intercourse*" (emphasis ours).[6] Leaders, you might very well be the *only* ones checking up on your teens, encouraging them in purity and in their walk with God. Keep communicating as much as possible, and if your group is so large that keeping up with communication is too much to handle alone, recruit help!

We know you can't change all your study lessons and discussion topics to purity exclusively, but you can reinforce the message of "Fearless Purity" through your next social media update, mass e-mail, or text blast.

SAMPLE MESSAGES

- How many of you were convicted about where your current relationships stand after last week's session?
- If you hope to get married, have you prayed for your future husband or wife today?
- What are your physical boundary lines? Do you have accountability?
- Have you lowered your standards this week? How did that make you feel?
- Have you made a purity pledge? What will help you stay committed to it?
- How are the movies you're watching affecting your goal to wait for what God has for you?
- Which story from your *Culture Shock* survival guide inspired you the most? Why?
- You've got a long-time crush whose standards are not so godly. What if he or she takes notice of you? What will you do?

Another follow-up idea is to have an old-school pizza party. Make it really casual for your teens, and talk with them as much as possible one-on-one or in small groups of three or four. It's important for teens to know how much you care about them personally and the choices they're making. Encourage them to communicate with you and their parents.

Use the following questions in your small groups or other gatherings, in either a casual conversation time or a more formal, organized discussion.

DISCUSSION QUESTIONS for GUYS

1. Guys, you are supposed to be the boundary enforcers. Have you set boundary lines in a relationship, only to cross them? Have you ever pushed your date to cross emotional, physical, or spiritual boundary lines you've set up?

A cool story from our team:

> Travis and Annie got into a relationship and knew they wanted to get married. Guess who was the one who wanted to save the first kiss for the wedding day. *Travis!* The guy! How cool is that?!
>
> In a culture that encourages guys to always demand more from girls, we are seeing a generation of young men willing to stand up and take the lead regarding purity. It is an incredible move of God, and we hope you will be a part of it!

2. How can you avoid making the mistakes of the past? Make a list of your "weak places" when you are with a date—alone in the car, in a dark theater, in your bedroom, or alone in an empty house. How can you plan to avoid these tempting spots?

3. Are you in a relationship—or is there someone you want to be in a relationship with? After the testimonies you've heard, do you feel this person is God's best for you? Why or why not?

4. Can you see how girls view being "good friends" differently from the way you do? Is there anything you should change about the way you treat or communicate with the girls around you?

5. Gut-check question, if it applies to you: How does pornography change the way you view women? How will it affect your future marriage if that is what shapes the way you view sex?

1. Have you set boundary lines in a relationship, only to cross them? Have you ever manipulated your date to cross emotional, physical, or spiritual boundary lines you've set up? (Think about the way you flirt, dress, talk, and act when you are with guys.)

2. If you have a boyfriend, let's say you leave this session and tell your boyfriend what you've learned. How do you think he'd react? Are you prepared to leave an unhealthy relationship you know isn't right?

3. What can you do to avoid entering into an unhealthy relationship in the first place?

4. Have you ever become attached to one of your guy friends? Can you see how guys view friendship differently from the way you do? How can you avoid becoming attached in the first place?

5. Gut-check question, if it applies to you: How does pornography change the way you view men? How will it affect your future marriage if that is what shapes the way you view sex?

BUILDING THE BRIDGE

Use the ideas below to connect with parents to make sure they know what their kids are being told regarding romantic relationships and sexual purity. We've also included ideas on helping parents connect with their teens about these issues. For more resources, including weekly parent updates and key resource recommendations, visit us online at www.generationsofvirtue.org.

OVERVIEW OF FEARLESS PURITY

Sexual purity is one of the biggest issues on the mind of every teen. Whether they've made positive or negative choices in this area, our goal is to get everyone headed in the same direction: purity of heart, mind, and body.

Sadly, there is so much cultural pressure bombarding our teens that this goal often seems impossible. However, in "Fearless Purity" we equipped the teens with practical, effective strategies and tools to stay pure and stand strong against the power that seeks to destroy their hearts, minds, and future relationships.

We explained to the teens that holding on to fearless purity is not just about denying themselves now for no reason; it's about sowing seeds that will reap tremendous benefits in the future. It's about honoring the life God has for them, and if marriage is in their plans, it's about honoring that future spouse and marriage—before it starts. And this fight for purity begins today.

Encourage your teen to make a solid evaluation of his or her physical boundaries. For more information, check out *Culture Shock: A Survival Guide for Teens*.

FIVE GREAT DISCUSSION POINTS FOR PARENTS AND TEENS

1. What do you think defines "purity of heart, mind, and body"? What does *purity* mean to you?

2. As you're moving further into your teens and twenties, what kinds of standards do you want to set up regarding purity in your life?

3. What do you think of dating? Do you think it has a place in your teen years? Why or why not?

4. Do you feel there is anything in your life right now that is compromising your purity? Can I help you work that out in any way?

5. In your future friendships and relationships, what kinds of boundaries can we set up in order to protect your purity?

CONNECT: AN ACTIVITY FOR PARENTS AND TEENS

During "Fearless Purity," your teen learned about the importance of living in a way that guards, protects, and honors his or her future *right now*. What a cool concept, huh? In order to build on that framework, we think you can reap great benefits by sitting down with your teen and encouraging him or her to write out a vision of future marriage. It could include very simple things, such as:

★ **I want to love and be loved.**

★ **I want to honor God and serve him.**

★ **I want to make a safe and healthy home for our family.**

★ **I want to walk in our God-given destiny.**

Now, take that list and go through it point by point. The idea is to get discussion going with your teen on *how* to obtain these things desired in marriage. Why not start preparing now? And if your teenager does not have marriage in mind, talk about how maintaining purity and integrity will affect whatever goals he or she may have.

Encourage your teen and any teens you know: If they want happy, healthy lives and loving marriages, they need to begin cultivating authentic love now. If they want healthy home environments, they need to learn healthy habits, boundaries, conflict resolution, and relational skills now. As a parent or as a friend to other teens you know, help them develop the areas that are most needed to accomplish their goals. It may seem odd, but it's never too early to start preparing teens for the future.

PLUG IN

Youth leaders should be sure to e-mail parents to communicate with them about what their teens have been discussing and learning. Feel free to send them the Overview of the session and the Five Great Discussion Points. Introduce them to the idea of the Connect activity as well. Include your contact information so parents can reach you if they have questions.

Make use of Facebook updates, Twitter messages, texts, and e-mail to send messages of encouragement and connection to parents of the teens you work with. If they don't use any of these forms of communication, find out what works best for them (a phone call, brief meetings). Just keep the communication lines open!

SAMPLE MESSAGES

- "Blessed are the pure in heart, for they will see God" (Matthew 5:8).
- Pray with your teen today about purity. What areas can you help with? What areas present a struggle?
- Do you have accountability software on your computers? Check out www .generationsofvirtue.org.

- Remember: Purity is worth fighting for!
- Consider asking your teen this: "Would you keep doing what you're doing if your future spouse were watching?"
- God's view of sex and culture's view of sex are completely different things. Ask your teen to explain the difference.

PART FIVE

ESCAPING NORMAL

There's a common trend we've noticed about teenagers all over the globe, no matter what nation we go to: Teens are constantly in search of the next latest and greatest thing. So much so that this prevailing mentality has seeped into every aspect of their lives—fashion, technology, appearance, language, mannerisms, and more. But it's more than constant change on superficial levels. We've noticed that there's very little, if any, consistency and commitment to accomplishing any certain task. Teens are characterized by a sort of restless fidgetiness—a phenomenon that parents have relegated to "normal teenage behavior."

Have you noticed this? Many teens bounce from one thing (activity, passion, friendship) to another. They flap around aimlessly like dandelions tossed here and there by a gust of wind. They wander around purposeless—space cowboys in search of the next big thrill. Their reasoning is this: "I saw this on television" or "That's what all the kids are doing these days." They thrive on short-lived adrenaline, with little vision for the future. Living in the moment is their life slogan. "Who cares about where I'll be in five years? I only care about what feels good right now. I'm living for today, and I'm gonna have fun while I'm at it!"

So what is their view of God? For many, it's this: *pfft*. He's this transcendent being that's really just *up there*. "I don't bug him—he doesn't have time for petty little things like my life and future. He has bigger things to worry about, and I'm definitely not one of them." Others might say, "Look around you! Clearly, God doesn't know what he's doing. He's slippin' on the job. I'm the master of my own destiny, so ummm . . . I guess that makes *me* god."

We've heard it all, and you probably have too.

The goal of this session is to help your teens understand the magnitude of God's call on their lives. The creator of the universe has a wonderful and intricate destiny for every one of them. Never for a second were they an afterthought, a freakish accident, or a second-rate creation.

We love what the Word of God says in Jeremiah 29:11 (*The Message*): "I know what I'm doing. I have it all planned out—plans to take care of you, not abandon you, plans to give you the future you hope for." It begins with the affirmation that God's in perfect control of the world and our lives. Nothing goes unnoticed. What an assurance that is! The verse goes on to say, essentially, that he has our lives planned out. He's a God of details. Like a director shooting a film, he has every scene and every shot outlined. The great news is this: the movie that he's directing is a guaranteed success. When teens let God sit in the director's chair of their lives, it's going to be incredible!

During the course of this event, your teens will be introduced to concepts such as God's mighty calling, servant leadership, keys to fulfilling their destiny, and what we call destiny stealers. So brace yourselves for a wild ride!

Before you dive into this session, take some time to:

★ **READ—Read through the session, of course, but also spend time in the Scriptures that are suggested throughout. Some of the main passages are: Proverbs 29:18; Jeremiah 1:6-9; 29:11; Mark 10:43-45; Romans 8:28; Ephesians 3:20; Philippians 4:13; and 1 Timothy 4:12. Read the surrounding verses or chapters of these passages so you are aware of the context.**

★ **WATCH—In the time leading up to your session or event, watch out for specific examples** in television shows, advertising, movies, video games, magazines, online content and elsewhere of messages aimed at teens about their destiny or purpose. Having these examples fresh in your mind may be helpful as you lead your group.

★ **PRAY—Ask God for wisdom for yourself and your fellow leaders. Pray for vision and passion as you lead discussions with your teens. Pray for specific girls and guys you know who need to hear this message.**

BREAKING IT DOWN

"Escaping Normal" is the final event in the Culture Shock program, and because of this you may wish to handle it slightly differently from the other event sessions. We recommend the following ideas:

1. Use this as a longer event by breaking it into three sessions:

★ **Session One: Share key points of Servant Leadership and an overview of "Escaping Normal." Then move into the Guess Who activity.**

★ **Session Two: Open with God's Mighty Calling and the discussion questions that go with that section. Do the Three Wishes**

activity. Close with Six Solomons and Keys to Living an Extraordinary Life.

★ **Session Three: Help teens realize their Destiny Stealers. Close session with Letters to God.**

2. Break into two sessions:

★ **Session One: Share key points of Servant Leadership and do the Guess Who activity. Close with God's Mighty Calling discussion questions.**

★ **Session Two: Begin with Three Wishes. Talk about Destiny Stealers. Close session with Letters to God.**

3. Use as a one-session event: Share key points about Servant Leadership and do the Guess Who activity. Talk about key points from God's Mighty Calling and do Three Wishes. Discuss Destiny Stealers. Close with Letters to God.

THE MAIN EVENT

Once you've decided how to organize your sessions, prepared yourself and your team, gathered your teens, and given it all over to God, you're ready to complete your Culture Shock journey!

SEND THIS MESSAGE

Make this loud and clear to your students from the start:

★ **God has a plan that he designed uniquely for you. Don't let your destiny get stolen!**

★ **The key to greatness and fulfilling God's calling on your life lies in serving. Apply this truth to your life—it will propel you to fulfilling your destiny.**

Here's a suggestion for opening the session with prayer:

Lord, I thank you so much for every young person in this room. Father, I ask that even now you would be preparing them to answer your call on their lives. You have awesome plans in store for this generation; we know that there is no way we can out-dream you and the destiny you have for each one of us. Father, I ask that you would give each person here a vision for the calling you have placed on their lives. Thank you, Lord, for opening their hearts and minds to receive your calling. In Jesus' name, amen.

SERVANT LEADERSHIP

It's very possible you have a teenager in your group who sits way in the back during meetings—disengaged and really not wanting to be there. Or maybe you're leading that teenager who wants to be the center of attention and feels that the world revolves around him or her. Or it could be that you're the mentor of that teen who loves Jesus with all of his or her heart.

No matter who they are or how they behave now, your teenagers need to know that the key to getting ahead is taking a lower position. One of the best ways to fulfill your destiny is to become a servant to others.

God has brought our team through seasons of pruning, teaching, and humbling. He's shown us the position that we are to adopt—namely that of a servant. The founders of our faith, the men and women of God who lived extraordinary lives, were great only because they were great servants. And the greatest servant of all was Jesus.

Read Mark 10:43-45 (*NLT*): "But among you it will be different. Whoever wants to be a leader among you must be your servant, and whoever wants to be first among you must be the slave of everyone else. For even the Son of Man came not to be served but to serve others and to give his life as a ransom for many."

KEY POINTS TO SHARE

★ **Teens need to gain a realistic view of what should be the focus of their time and energy as they prepare for their destiny in Christ. Young people are often encouraged to snatch up whatever leadership positions they can get their hands on and pad their résumés as much as possible in order to get themselves on the road to achievement. But God's training is different. Instead of rewards or honors or certifications, he asks us to acquire humility, mercy, and compassion.**

★ God alone knows what the future holds for you, and he alone will know the best way to prepare for that future. Many leaders in ministry share this feeling: "I had all these plans laid out for my life, but then God called me to the ministry, and it was so not what I expected to be doing; I was not prepared for this." God knows where you are headed and how to prepare you for that path, even though you may not be aware of it.

★ Servant leadership is a critical part of the training all teens and young adults will need in order to fulfill their call. As Robert K. Greenleaf put it in his essay "The Servant as Leader" (1970): "The servant leader *is* servant first."

This next activity was designed with today's youth in mind, to aid them in wanting to serve and follow God with all their hearts, minds, and bodies. This is no ordinary calling, and it will require no ordinary training. They will need to rely on the Lord to know what to do and when to do it. Teens today have an extraordinary calling—let's prepare them accordingly.

ACTIVITY: GUESS WHO

This activity is set up like a game show. Teens accumulate points by guessing the name of a famous missionary or Christian leader. For each round, players will hear a set of statements written from the perspective of the mystery person. The statements will be delivered one at a time, and the first person to guess the name of the mystery person wins the points for that round. Only one person can answer at a time, so players will have to beat the other players to the answer. The team or individual with the most points at the end wins.

Goal: To help students realize that their history is part of their destinies! God will use all their experiences for his glory when they turn their lives over to him. The Word says: "We know that in all things God works for the good of those who love him, who have been called according to his purpose" (Romans 8:28).

LEADER TIP

Provide some kind of signal the team or individual must give when they want to answer. This can be as simple as raising a hand or a brightly colored flag. Feel free to get creative with it! Another idea is to place a bell in the middle of the room. Have all your teens or teams positioned an equal distance from the bell. Once the question is read, the first person or group leader to run to the bell and ring it gets to answer the question.

Here are our suggested rounds. Some are harder than others, which is why they're worth more points. After each mystery person is revealed, talk about the impact he or she had on the kingdom of God. When you see how their lives began, it's incredible to think of what God has done through them!

LEADER TIP

Feel free to add in your own staff to this game. If your group is tightly knit and knows you or the leadership of your church or ministry well, consider making someone from your team one of the mystery people. Make sure to include menial jobs the person has had or humbling tidbits, as the point of the game is to show your students that even the most famous Christian leaders had a time of preparation that usually included hard or humble circumstances.

100 POINTS

I'm the youngest of eight children.

I brought food to troops during war.

I spent hours playing music and writing worship songs.

I was a shepherd for the majority of my young life.

Answer: David, king of Israel[7]

Additional info: Called "a man after God's heart." He went on to lead Israel into countless victorious battles and write many of the psalms. His son Solomon built the temple in Jerusalem, but only after David set up the whole operation.

200 POINTS

I lived with my parents long into my adult years.

I spent a year in a prison camp.

I was a watchmaker for more than twenty years.

I hid people from authorities in the attic of my house.

Answer: Corrie Ten Boom[8]

Additional info: Corrie was an evangelist and watchmaker from Holland who stayed pretty well unnoticed by society until she started hiding Jews in her house during the Nazi occupation of Holland during World War II. She hid seven Jews in her house attic, but she was the organizer of an entire ring of Amsterdam households hiding Jews. Corrie procured ration cards (necessary to buy food for the hidden Jews) for homes all over Holland. It is estimated that Corrie and her family saved the lives of more than 800 Jews through their underground work. Corrie, her father, and her sister Betsie were sent to a concentration camp. After coming out of the camp, Corrie ministered to thousands of people all around the world (including the German people) through her speaking and writing. Her most famous work is called *The Hiding Place*.

200 POINTS

> I preached to the poor in an open-air market.
>
> I studied medicine for two years, but never got my degree.
>
> The first offer of marriage that I made was rejected.
>
> I spent most of my life bankrupt.
>
> I almost died sailing from England to China.

Answer: Hudson Taylor[9]

Additional info: Founder of the China Inland Mission. Taylor proposed to his girlfriend, but was rejected because she did not want to move to China. He faced numerous challenges in that country, ministering during a volatile time in Chinese history. He also lost numerous children and his wife to death. Yet the impact of his ministry led more than 125,000 Chinese to Christ in the mid-nineteenth century. His ministry was the single most widely reaching ministry in China at the time. Because of the seeds he and others planted, the church in China today is thriving and growing more than ever before.

100 POINTS

> My mother was forced to abandon me as an infant after the government threatened my life.
>
> I was convicted of murder.
>
> I gave up wealth and membership in a prestigious family to answer God's call.
>
> I spent forty years watching sheep in the desert.

Answer: Moses[10]

Additional info: He led the Israelites out of slavery in Egypt and eventually toward the promised land. He was a faithful shepherd who freed an entire nation, then led them for forty years through the desert. There are historians who believe that Moses was one of the greatest leaders in history.

300 POINTS

I attended three different Bible colleges before I graduated from Moody with a degree in anthropology.

I wanted to be a chaplain in the armed forces, but I got the mumps.

I was the president of Northwestern College for four years.

I used circus tents for my first big revival meeting.

Answer: Billy Graham[11]

Additional info: Said to have reached more than 200 million people for Christ. A passionate revivalist who sided with Martin Luther King Jr. during the civil rights movement in the U.S., Graham's relationship with his wife was one of his most important priorities. Most of his adult life has been spent in the spotlight. Because of this, he made sure the public knew he was faithful to his wife. One of the ways he did this was by always having a friend check his hotel room before he retired after a long day of ministering, just to confirm a woman wasn't in there with the intention of ruining his reputation.

100 POINTS

I was labeled an illegitimate child while growing up.

I was not formally educated.

I was only in public ministry for three years—before I was killed.

I was a carpenter until I was about thirty years old.

Answer: Jesus[12]

Additional info: One with God, he was there in the beginning of creation (Colossians 1:16), yet became human and lived among us. He called himself Living Water, the Bread of Life, and the Light of the World, among other names. He died on a cross and rose from the dead to bring salvation to all people so that anyone who believes in him can come to the Father.

300 POINTS

I was shot in the ankle when serving in the Dutch army.

I spent a lot of time when I was young taking care of my invalid mother and my brother, who was mentally handicapped.

I spent two years working in a chocolate factory.

I couldn't afford toothpaste when I attended a Bible college in Glasgow, Scotland.

The first car I used to take Bibles behind the Iron Curtain was donated to me.

Answer: Brother Andrew[13]

Additional info: Missionary to the Soviet-controlled states in Eastern Europe during the 1950s and '60s, Brother Andrew smuggled Bibles into Communist countries where it was either illegal to own a Bible or severely dangerous to be a Christian. Brother Andrew's organization, Open Doors, now spreads the Word of God to more than sixty closed nations. Brother Andrew and Open Doors have smuggled millions of Bibles all over the world, with one single mission to China having brought one million Bibles at one time.

100 POINTS

I was an orphan.

My family was taken captive by invaders of my homeland.

I was forced to live in a king's palace.

I became queen over this foreign people.

I pleaded for my life and the lives of my people before the king.

Answer: Esther[14]

Additional info: Despite being a captive in Persia, Esther rose to the position of queen, thanks in large part to the wisdom of her relative, Mordecai. She kept her ancestry hidden until she pleaded for the lives of the Jews before the king. She was able to save the Jews by her obedience. The Jews still celebrate the life of Esther today, during the holiday called Purim.

200 POINTS

> I worked with the homeless for years in my native country.
>
> I never married, but I had hundreds of children.
>
> I worked for fifty-six years against an oppressive class system.
>
> I died in the land God called me to. My children wrote "Amma" on my grave.

Answer: Amy Carmichael[15]

Additional info: Started orphanages in India, helping children who were to be given as slaves to local temples—children destined by their culture to be temple prostitutes or live other degrading lives. Amy lived and ministered in India fifty-six years. She fought against the unjust caste system of India, rescuing children otherwise doomed to a horrible existence.

200 POINTS

> I started working as a maid in England at fourteen.
>
> I was turned down by a missionary board because I was poorly educated.
>
> I knew God was sending me to a foreign land when I was eighteen, but I
>   didn't get to go until I was almost thirty.
>
> In China, I served hungry travelers: providing meals, lodging, and the gospel.

Answer: Gladys Aylward[16]

Additional info: Denied by the China Inland Mission, Gladys knew God had called her to China. After working for several years as a maid, she traveled to China by train through war-torn Russia because she couldn't afford a ticket for a ship. Once in China, she and another missionary started an inn for travelers, using the opportunity of having travelers under their roof to preach the gospel.

100 POINTS

> I was the victim of cruel bullies in boarding school.
>
> I was a soldier in WWI.
>
> Earlier in my life, I was a staunch atheist.
>
> I spent twenty-nine years at Oxford.

Answer: C. S. Lewis[17]

Additional info: He authored some of the most famous English literary works: *The Chronicles of Narnia*, *Mere Christianity*, *The Screwtape Letters*, and many others. When he set out to disprove the existence of God intellectually, Lewis became a Christian and then spent the rest of his life putting words to the theology he continued to explore.

FOR SMALL GROUPS

If your group is small enough, have everyone participate in the game individually.

FOR WEEKEND RETREATS

To involve everyone in a larger group, break the group into teams, and appoint a spokesperson who will answer for the team. Think *Family Feud* game show style: this sets up a team and teamwork approach to the game. The spokespersons can all stand in front of their teams so you can identify them easily.

FOR CAMPS

See note above about using spokespersons. Or, if you have a large outdoor or indoor space to work with, it might actually be more fun to break into teams and then let anyone on a team who knows the answer give the answer (only one person per team at a time), except that they have to run and touch a target or grab a flag (placed some distance away) before they can give an answer. This adds an extra active element to the game.

When the Guess Who game is finished, move directly into personal testimony about a servant position you have held or a seemingly pointless job you have taken, and how God used that position to teach you something for your current ministry.

A sample story from our team:

> From Megan: During my last semester of college, I was looking for a part-time, on-campus job. I prayed and prayed for a week or so, but still didn't feel any peace about any of the positions I had applied for: professor's assistant, library attendant, and an after-school program director at an elementary school. I thought one of those jobs was surely the job God had for me. I mean, they would all look really good on my résumé. I was pretty confident I'd get one of them—especially the assistant position,

because the professor himself had asked me to apply for it. But I still was seeking God about which job to take.

The curveball came when I got an e-mail announcing job openings. The facilities services department needed janitor's assistants—people who cleaned dorms. I very distinctly heard the Lord tell me to take the job. I was incredulous! Surely this is not what God had for me. But the nudge continued. I couldn't deny he was telling me to take the job I least desired. This job choice was social suicide—not to mention not helpful for the kind of professional reputation I was trying to build. Janitor's assistants at my school were kind of looked on as the lepers of the college community. You would be extremely unfortunate if you had to accept this job—usually only unknowing freshmen took it after they failed to snatch up the jobs at the coffee shop, admissions office, or even the dining hall. On the totem pole of campus jobs, janitor's assistant was definitely at the very bottom.

So I started this job with a sense of dread. The first few shifts were hard, and to be honest I did not have a good attitude. Not only did I get dirty as I scrubbed disgusting shower stalls and crawled around on my hands and knees picking up last night's pizza party leftovers in the lounge, but it was also humiliating when freshmen and sophomores would walk by wondering how I—a senior—had the misfortune to take this job.

However, by my third shift, something strange started to happen. I started enjoying myself. I got to work on my own, which was no small thing considering my over-packed, highly socialized schedule. Cleaning became a break in my busy day, when I had the opportunity to connect with God. God spoke to me more during those two hours of cleaning every day than at any other time during my college career. I grew to love that job because it was my time with God. And when I was honest with myself, I realized I also actually enjoyed cleaning.

I now look back on that janitor's assistant job with great fondness. I'm so glad God told me to take that position. Not only did I thoroughly enjoy it, it also gave me an opportunity to minister to people. I was constantly praying for opportunities to share the gospel during college, and this job gave me inside access to the places where students lived, talked with each other, and struggled with deep issues. They would talk to me because I was approachable. Surely the person who took the janitor's assistant job was not going to judge or belittle them as they shared their fears and struggles. I was able to share with and pray for people who wouldn't be caught dead at a campus Bible study or a worship service, simply because of the job I had.

This experience taught me that the Lord's ways are truly magnificent. He answers prayers in ways we would least expect it. More importantly, when he tells you to take a low position—take it! He knows what he's doing.

GOD'S MIGHTY CALLING

This generation has often been proclaimed as having the greatest potential. The reality is that potential, unharnessed, remains *nothing but potential*. Your task as a leader is to help your teens see a vision for their lives that far exceeds where they are now. A great leadership expert, John Maxwell, notes that successful people are visionaries. They are individuals who can see the big picture for their lives. A leader, on the other hand, is one who helps others see and fulfill their vision and calling—God's awesome plan and purpose.

It may be that you've seen your teens running around with little or no purpose in life. God is a God of destiny and purpose. He never operates by chance or accident. He has an incredible call for every teen in your group.

Help the teens of this generation fulfill their potential. Help them walk in God's destiny for their lives. They need a visionary leader—they need you.

"Where there is no vision, the people perish" (Proverbs 29:18, *KJV*). The bottom line is this: your teens will perish spiritually if they're not pursuing the calling, destiny, and vision that God has for their lives. On the one hand, this reality is alarming, given the weight of responsibility that's placed on our shoulders. But it opens up a world of opportunities to impact this generation and the following generations for God's glory.

Sit down with your leadership team to pray, discuss, and brainstorm about the direction you're heading as a youth group and youth leadership team. People need to know where you're going. When your teens see your vision, it'll take them in the right direction toward pursuing their God-given destiny. Until your leadership team accomplishes this, you leave the door open for assumption, misunderstanding, discord, and unclear and unmet expectations within your team and youth group.

DISCUSSION QUESTIONS FOR ALL

As a place to start, consider these questions first with your leadership team before this event happens. Then during the event, take time to sit down with groups of teens and discuss these questions:

1. What are our goals as a youth group?

2. What do we stand for?

3. What is the vision—God's vision—for our youth group? What verses of the Bible can help us understand God's vision for us?

4. What are we hoping to accomplish in the next six months? three years?

5. What is our long-term vision for the group?

6. What role do you think you will play in the growth of this group?

ACTIVITY: THREE WISHES

This activity is highly discussion driven and is most effective when the group is broken down into smaller groups. The suggested size of each group is five to twelve teens. Participation is key to the success of the activity.

SUPPLIES NEEDED

- ★ **Sticky notes (three per teen)**
- ★ **Pens or pencils**
- ★ **Tape**
- ★ **Butcher paper or other large blank paper (seven sheets)**

Each small group is assigned a leader. The leader reads The Scenario to the group, and everyone is given three to five minutes to think of responses and write them on sticky notes—one wish per note. At the end, each member takes turns sharing his or her answers. Your teenagers' responses should fall under one of seven categories our team has identified. Assign each sheet of butcher paper one category, labeling each at the top. The seven categories are:

- ★ **Money and Success**
- ★ **Fame, Attention, and Recognition**
- ★ **Power and Control**
- ★ **Independence and Freedom from Authority**
- ★ **Appearance and Reputation**
- ★ **Love and Relationships**
- ★ **Things of Eternal Value**

Once labeled, attach the seven sheets to a wall. You can place them side by side, but make sure students are *not* able to see the categories (fold the sheets in half and tape the bottom halves over the tops, covering the labels). Your teens will be attaching their sticky notes onto the butcher paper later in the activity.

Once the students have arrived at the activity area, divide them into groups (or use the same groups from a previous activity). Let everyone sit in a circle. If these groups are new, just make certain all the members know one another's names. Pass out the sticky notes and pens or pencils before you begin reading.

THE SCENARIO

It's the night before you leave for college. You're extremely nervous—to the brink of having a panic attack. It's just dawned on you that you're about to leave everything you know and love—your parents, siblings, hometown, high school, youth group, and friends. You're the firstborn, and going to college is a huge step for both you and your family. The expectations are overwhelming. You're frozen in time, terrified by the idea that the outcome of your future rests on the next four years of your life.

Stuck in the rubble of suitcases, boxes, small appliances, and farewell cards, an angel of the Lord appears to you in the middle of your room. You are shocked—you don't know what to do! As if you weren't already nervous, now you feel like you've totally lost your mind. Before you can run away, the angel introduces himself, saying he brings with him a message from the Lord. Here's how the message reads:

> *Dear Child of God,*
>
> *I am completely aware of the transition to college that you're about to make. I know this because this is a small part of my awesome plan for your life. To help you ease into this new season of your life, I hereby grant you three wishes. You may ask anything that your heart desires, and I will grant it to you.*
>
> *Peace and Love,*
>
> *Your Heavenly Father*

After reading the scenario, leaders, encourage your teens to write down their three wishes on the sticky notes provided—one wish per note. Then take turns sharing wishes with the group. Be sure to include the reasons behind your wishes.

A note to leaders: Often in Christian circles, students will give "spiritual" answers to the Three Wishes activity. A question to think about: what is their motivation behind this? If they are truly, wholeheartedly following after God, then great! But many times, students will give the answers that "look" the best to the leaders. Encourage your teens to be completely honest during this activity; it will make all the difference in the end.

Once everyone has shared, introduce the seven categories of wishes to the whole group. Unfold the butcher paper one sheet at a time to reveal the categories. Then instruct your teens to attach their sticky notes onto the butcher paper corresponding to the category that best fits each wish.

Leaders, be ready to provide assistance in identifying which categories their wishes most accurately fall under. Important! Let students know there are no "wrong" categories. For instance, if it seems obvious the best match is, say, Fame, Attention, and Recognition, encourage them to post their answer there. No one is going to be called out for choosing "less spiritual" answers!

DISCUSSION QUESTIONS FOR ALL

Now have an open discussion that all students can participate in. Here are some suggested questions to consider:

1. What do the majority of your wishes revolve around? Material possessions, wealth, popularity, and other superficial desires? Or are they about other things, such as compassion, wisdom, grace, and loving others?

2. Why do you think this is the case?

3. Are you more interested in stuff that brings temporary satisfaction and instant gratification? Or are you more concerned with things that are of eternal value?

4. If you were to present your three wishes to God, would he be pleased with them? What do you think his response would be?

5. Do your wishes advance God's kingdom? How could they do so?

6. Do your wishes help fulfill God's calling and destiny for your life? How could they do so?

FOR SMALL GROUPS

If your group size is fewer than twelve, feel free to just stay together as one group. Or you could break groups up into girl and guy groups, if you think that might be beneficial.

FOR WEEKEND RETREATS

Break your teens up into smaller groups of five to twelve teens. You can use the same groups assigned for the Guess Who activity or you can reassign group-ings. Some ideas for assignment methods: by age, month of birthday, favorite color, and so on.

WHY SETTLE FOR NORMAL?

Leaders, this is your chance to drive home the messages of this and all the Culture Shock events. Engage your teens in a discussion of normal vs. extraordinary.

Have you noticed that everything God does is extraordinary? Not quite convinced? Think Genesis 1 and 2, just to name an example. The omnipo-tent God of the universe formed and fashioned everything in our world from nothing. Now, fast-forward many thousands of years. God sends his Son, Jesus, to redeem humanity. And like his Father, Jesus too performed extraordi-nary feats over his three-year period of recorded ministry—making something from nothing.

Think about the miracles he performed: healing people who were blind, deaf, lame, and mute; turning water into wine; feeding thousands on someone's lunch; walking on water; raising people from death to life; and, of course, his own incredible resurrection, allowing us all to be freed from the slavery of sin. There's not even the slightest hint of normal in any of those acts. *Normal* just does not exist in the vocabulary of Heaven.

Let's think about what normal means. What other words would you use for *normal*? (Let teens shout out answers.)

Some examples:

* **standard**
* **ordinary**
* **typical**
* **common**
* **everyday**

* **customary**
* **conventional**
* **boring**

Are these the sorts of words you would like used to describe your calling and purpose? More to the point, would God characterize your destiny along these lines? The answer is a resounding NO. Why would the supreme God of the universe destine you for ordinary when ordinary does not exist in him?

Settling for anything less than God's plan for our lives is not only unwise, it's a direct insult to God. If we settle, we reject God's call and purpose and accept what the world offers. And if we do that, we can be sure that at some point the God of the universe will ask us: "Why settle for normal when you can be extraordinary?"

SIX SOLOMONS

To illustrate this point, let's examine the life of King Solomon, whose story is found in the Old Testament, in 1 Kings 3. Does anyone know anything about King Solomon? (Let teens shout out answers. For example: he was granted wisdom from God, he had a lot of wives, he was a king of Israel, he wrote the book of Proverbs, he was the son of David, and so on. Praise teens for the answers they are able to give correctly.) Use the six points below to cover the major events of his life.

For a fun and creative twist, choose six volunteers to act as "Solomons." Ask the volunteers to stand in a line facing the audience. Number them from one to six. Read point number one aloud, then instruct the first person to act out the fact that you just said. Then go to number two, then three, etc.

1. Solomon became Israel's king after his father David.

2. God visited Solomon one night in a dream. God presented Solomon with the opportunity to ask for anything he desired, and whatever he asked would be granted to him.

3. Solomon asked for wisdom.

4. Solomon was endowed with a supernatural measure of wisdom.

5. Solomon's fame grew and Israel became prosperous during his reign.

6. In addition to that—and to honor Solomon because he did not ask for wealth—God also gave him more riches and wealth than any other man alive!

(Allow the six Solomons to go back to their seats.)

If you're now saying "Great! He lived happily ever after!"—wait up just a second. When you read 1 Kings 3, you'll realize there's more than meets the eye with this story. Solomon ascended to the throne of Israel after his father David, who was unquestionably Israel's greatest king. If that wasn't daunting enough, picture an inexperienced young lad anointed as king over not just any nation, but the nation known as the chosen people of God.

The boy was way out his league and he knew it! Solomon lamented in 1 Kings 3:7, 8, "Now, LORD my God, you have made your servant king in place of my father David. But I am only a little child and do not know how to carry out my duties. Your servant is here among the people you have chosen, a great people, too numerous to count or number."

This was your perfect recipe for failure, one of those situations where you throw your hands up in the air and say, "God, I sure hope you know what you're doing." Ever been there?

But this is exactly the sort of thing that God does. He's in the business of transforming the normal in our lives into something extraordinary. He's looking for individuals who are willing to embrace the amazing destiny that God has for them, no matter where they are in life. If you feel that you have nothing to offer the kingdom, look out—you're in the perfect position to be used by God. Remember, you are never too young or too old to pursue God's incredible calling on your life.

The Bible gives us countless examples of men and women who were young and inexperienced when God took hold of their lives. Think of Esther, Samuel, David, Gideon, Joseph, and Timothy, just to name a few. God brought each of them on an amazing journey where their callings and destinies were fulfilled. His only requirement for each of them was an obedient and undivided heart.

Back to Solomon . . . Faced with the intimidating task of having to lead a kingdom, Solomon requested wisdom so he could better lead God's people with integrity and justice. Not the kind of response you'd typically hear from a young person—let alone a king. In a period when kings coveted riches, honor, recognition, victorious military campaigns, expansion of territory, and much more, Solomon asked for wisdom. Scripture tells us that God was so pleased with Solomon's request, he not only granted Solomon wisdom, but he blessed Solomon with the stuff that he did not ask for—riches, honor, and success.

KEYS TO LIVING AN EXTRAORDINARY LIFE

★ **You serve a big God who desires for you to do big things. Dream big dreams. If God has given you the vision, then he'll also give you the ability to carry it out. Read Ephesians 3:20, Philippians 4:13, and Jeremiah 29:11.**

★ **Start pursuing God's purpose for your life right now. You're never too young or too old to start. Read Jeremiah 1:6-9 and 1 Timothy 4:12.**

★ **Build God's kingdom, not your own. Read Matthew 6:33.**

★ **Find someone to whom you can be accountable. Talk to him or her about your calling and purpose on a regular basis. Allow the person to speak into your life and mentor you as you pursue your calling. Read Proverbs 12:15.**

★ **Be teachable and glean from the wisdom of those who are older and wiser. Read 1 Peter 5:5.**

★ **Pursue a life of purity and holiness. Get lots of input from those older and wiser than you.**

ESCAPING NORMAL—CHALLENGE FOR LEADERS

Leaders, your mandate is to help your teens see, discern, and apprehend God's vision for their lives. Empower them to dream big for God. Motivate them to pursue their destinies now, not later in life. Loose the chains of limitations that society (and sometimes the church) has placed on them, so that they may be released into the fullness of their destinies.

Think of your role as that of an architect. Architects and designers have a unique ability to see the end product even while it's still in the works.

The task might appear to be beyond you at first, but know that as you remain connected to Christ Jesus, you'll be given the ability to discern God's plan for your students. You'll receive God's perspective to help your teens see the big picture of his calling on their lives. You'll obtain the grace to cultivate their giftedness and spur them on toward fulfilling their destinies.

REFLECTION QUESTIONS FOR LEADERS

In order to effectively empower your teens to fulfill their calling and destiny, you must first be walking according to God's plan and purpose for your life. You'd be surprised at the number of youth leaders and pastors we meet who have no idea why they do the things they do. If you haven't given much thought to your calling or aren't quite certain of your purpose and destiny, it's not too late to pursue God regarding these things. Reflect on these questions as they pertain to your calling and ministry:

1. What is my ultimate purpose in life? What am I here for?

2. What is God's vision for my life?

3. What are the deepest desires that God has placed in my heart? Am I endeavoring to accomplish them?

4. What is the vision that the Lord has given me for the group of teens I'm leading?

5. What are my motives and motivations for leading this group? Is it a paycheck, the recognition, the desire to be heard or to be famous—or other things? Where do my motives come from?

6. Am I truly invested in helping this generation fulfill God's calling for their lives? If not, what are some ways that I can invest myself in this generation? If yes, how can I give more of myself to help my teens succeed?

ACTIVITY: DESTINY STEALERS

Introduce this activity to the students with something like this: With God on your side, you have what it takes to live an extraordinary life. You can fulfill your calling and destiny. However, there are other things on the move that would try with all their might to destroy the lives of those pursuing the Lord in this generation. We identified some of these as categories in the Three Wishes activity. We call these destiny stealers. Let's examine them further.

Leaders: One way to handle this section would be to divide your teens into seven groups, one for each category. Appoint an adult leader for each group who will present the talking points and ask the discussion questions. For maximum effectiveness, we recommend that you enlist the help of adult volunteers, youth leaders, or members of your pastoral staff to facilitate and moderate the discussions. After enough time has passed, bring all the groups together and let a spokesperson from each tell about the main thoughts of that group's discussion. Leaders, be sure to wrap up after each category is presented.

MONEY AND SUCCESS. Someone once said, "Success is knowing God's destiny for your life and walking in it." The question is, do you want God's version of success or the world's?

DISCUSSION QUESTIONS ON MONEY AND SUCCESS

1. How would you describe the world's vision of success?

2. Are you the lord over your money or is your money lord over you?

3. How much money would make you happy? How much is enough?

4. Can money and success ever be used to advance God's kingdom? How?

5. Can money and success ever keep you from living out your calling and destiny? How?

6. Scripture point to consider: "Keep your life free from love of money and be content with what you have, because God has said, 'Never will I leave you; never will I forsake you'" (Hebrews 13:5). What do you think about this warning?

7. Does God want you to get rid of all your stuff? Read 1 Timothy 6:10 for further insight on this question.

8. God has given us a wonderful promise in Matthew 6:33: "But seek first his kingdom and his righteousness, and all these things will be given to you as well." What does the promise of this verse mean to you?

FAME, ATTENTION, AND RECOGNITION. A servant leader is not one who seeks fame, attention, and recognition. A servant leader serves with no expectation of receiving anything in return. Philippians 2:5-9 says of Jesus: "In your relationships with one another, have the same mind-set as Christ Jesus: Who, being in very nature God, did not consider equality with God something to be used to his own advantage; rather, he made himself nothing by taking the very nature of a servant, being made in human likeness. And being found in appearance as a man, he humbled himself by becoming obedient to death—even death on a cross!" Jesus humbled himself and made himself nothing. What an incredible testament of his willingness to fulfill his destiny and purpose for coming to earth. Are you willing to take a position of humility, like Jesus?

DISCUSSION QUESTIONS ON FAME, ATTENTION, AND RECOGNITION

1. Are you concerned about being the most popular person at school? Why or why not?

2. Does it bother you when your friends ignore you? Explain.

3. Do you get offended when you're not acknowledged or recognized for your efforts? Why?

4. What are your motives for seeking recognition and attention?

5. But he gives us more grace. That is why Scripture says: 'God opposes the proud but shows favor to the humble'" (James 4:6). What do you think of this statement: humility is an essential ingredient to fulfilling your destiny?

6. What do you think makes the world take notice? What does the world consider extraordinary?

7. How does God's version of extraordinary differ from what gets attention in the world? What examples have you seen of this?

POWER AND CONTROL. Don't let your desire to control the situations in your life derail you from God's path. Although you might describe it as just liking details and needing to know what's going on, often these are excuses for a person who wants to control everything. Sit back, relax, and let God control the show. You'll have a much more comfortable and happy ride along the way. "No one from the east or the west or from the desert can exalt themselves. It is God who judges: He brings one down, he exalts another" (Psalm 75:6, 7).

DISCUSSION QUESTIONS ON POWER AND CONTROL

1. Whether outwardly spoken or inwardly acknowledged, do you have a desire to control people and situations?

2. Do you always have to voice your opinion? When things don't go your way, do you get ticked? How do you think this kind of attitude helps you live out God's will? Or not?

3. How do you see people affected by a desire for power and control?

4. How do you see others affected by another person's desire for power and control over them?

5. When is it helpful to have power and control in terms of advancing the kingdom of God?

6. What about the need for power and control makes it difficult to deal with other people in the kingdom of God?

7. What attributes or character qualities could you work on in order to combat a need for power and control?

8. How could giving up power actually make you stronger?

INDEPENDENCE AND AUTHORITY. We've all served under leaders that we felt were less than ideal. Whether it was a pastor, teacher, boss, or parent, it's safe to say that we have all thought, *I just wish I could be my own boss!* Too often, we view bosses and authority figures as real pains, like constant roadblocks in the way of our fun. Let's take this up a notch and make this even more personal.

DISCUSSION QUESTIONS on INDEPENDENCE and AUTHORITY

1. Have you ever wished that you were born to a different family? Have you ever wished you had cooler parents or maybe someone else's parents? Why or why not?

2. Why is it critical to have authority in the world? Do you think humans were designed to govern themselves? Explain your answers.

3. Even Christ himself was subject to a higher authority, God the Father. Check out his prayer in the garden of Gethsemane—he *asked* God to take his cup from him (in other words, to spare him from dying on the cross). He didn't *tell* him (Matthew 26:39). What does this say to you?

4. Safety. Accountability. Consequences. What do these concepts have to do with authority? How much do these concepts come from having independence?

5. What are the pros and cons of having independence?

6. What are the pros and cons of living under authority?

7. How does serving those in authority, even if you don't agree with them always, advance the kingdom of God?

8. Romans 13:1 says, "Let everyone be subject to the governing authorities, for there is no authority except that which God has established." What do you think of this verse?

APPEARANCE AND REPUTATION. It seems most of our generation has lost the desire to appear good, holy, pure, and righteous before God. Teenagers are more concerned about looking good in the eyes of their peers than in the eyes of God. Young people torture themselves because they're not taller, slimmer, better looking, or just like that celebrity they idolize. They're constantly striving to be someone they're not. And some of them will do whatever it takes to make the fantasy a reality.

DISCUSSION QUESTIONS on APPEARANCE and REPUTATION

1. On a daily basis, what would you say—when you get up in the morning, do you think more about how you'll look in front of your friends, or how you'll look before God? Why do you think this is?

2. "Some of them will do whatever it takes to make the fantasy a reality." What do you think of that statement? How true is that among the teens you know? Will they take risks to save a reputation or maintain their image? What kind of risks?

3. How can a desire to look good and be well thought of be a good and healthy thing?

4. How can a desire to look good and be well thought of be a hindrance to following God's will for your life? Have you seen examples of this happening?

5. Have you ever, or known someone who has, hurt others in order to make yourself look better in front of your friends or people you wanted to impress? How did you feel about this?

6. What do you think would be God's version of cool? How would this be different from the world's version?

7. You were created in the image of God. He made you exactly as he desires you to be. And he loves you just the way you are. How does knowing these truths make a difference to you?

8. Legendary college basketball coach John Wooden once said, "Be more concerned with your character than your reputation, because your character is what you really are, while your reputation is merely what others think you are."[18] What do you think of this quote?

LOVE AND RELATIONSHIPS. The draw to be loved and the desire for a "perfect romance" can often become our number one goal while we're young. We've seen it in so many books, movies, and TV shows since we were little kids—by the time we hit our teen years we want to experience whatever they've claimed is so good! But now, more than any other time in your life, needs to be filled with getting to know Jesus Christ, learning to love him, and seeking his will for your life. God cares more about your love life than you could ever imagine!

DISCUSSION QUESTIONS ON LOVE AND RELATIONSHIPS

1. Why do you think teens are so obsessed with dating and romance? What is it they are looking for?

2. Do you think God doesn't want you to experience romance? Explain.

3. Think about this statement: "If you pursue relationships with a creature before you know and understand the creator, you will be frustrated and disappointed every single time." Do you agree or disagree with this statement? Why?

4. How can love get in the way of you knowing and understanding God's will for your life?

5. How can love help you understand God's will for your life?

6. I think we'd all agree that most teenage romances don't work out. If that is true, why do you think we are so intent on pursuing them? How can evaluating our needs for love and relationships help us to not depend on them so much?

7. Do you find it hard to trust God with your relationships? Why or why not?

8. How can focusing on Jesus and his love for you help you deal better with relationships?

THINGS OF ETERNAL VALUE. These—and not destiny stealers—are the things that you should desire and be pursuing. You may be wondering, *What are things of eternal value?* Things of eternal value are simply the attributes, characteristics, traits, virtues, mannerisms, thought patterns, and giftings that, when used to bring glory to God, benefit others and advance God's kingdom. These are attributes that are inherent in God himself and almost always cannot be bought with money. Some examples include: love, compassion, patience, wisdom, discernment, grace, a forgiving heart, kindness, goodness, humility, tolerance, being considerate, joy, love, peace, faith, generosity, meekness, self-control, and gentleness. (See Galatians 5:22, 23.)

DISCUSSION QUESTIONS ON THINGS OF ETERNAL VALUE

1. How do you or I get these things? (Read Matthew 7:7, 8.)

2. Though no one would argue that things in the lists above are good things, sometimes it's hard to see them in our lives. How do you see these things of eternal value in your life or in the lives of others?

3. How can a desire for some of the destiny stealers we have been talking about interfere with your ability to cultivate these things of eternal value?

4. Does God want you to get rid of stuff in your life so you can have more things of eternal value? What do you think?

5. What are some practical ways that you can practice the eternal qualities mentioned above?

YOUR VIEW

Can you think of other destiny stealers that plague your group? Feel free to come up with a list that is unique for your crew:

After all the groups have presented their thoughts on the destiny stealers, ask the group to think about these questions together in their smaller groups:

1. Which destiny stealers provide the biggest temptations for you?

2. How can you help each other overcome these destiny stealers?

ACTIVITY: LETTERS TO GOD

This activity serves not only as a closing for this session but also as a closing for the entire Culture Shock event series. This activity could serve as a great opportunity for parents to come to support their teens.

SUPPLIES NEEDED
* **paper, envelopes, and pens (enough for each student)**
* **stamps**

Youth leaders should pass out a sheet of paper, a pen, and an envelope to each student. Ask the teens to write a letter to God, thanking him and talking to him about everything they've learned during Culture Shock, and everything he's been teaching them, period! We encourage the teens to share these things with the Lord:

* **The promises they made during this time, such as "I want to be pure," "I want to guard my heart against lust," and "I want to pursue God's destiny for my life."**

* **Lifestyle patterns they want to change (examples: changing their group of friends, guarding against porn).**

* **How they want their lives to look in the future.**

If you have a worship band, you might ask them to play soft, worshipful music during this time. After the teens have written their letters, tell them to address the envelope to themselves, place the letter in the envelope, and seal it. Afterward, have a youth leader collect the letters.

In thirty days, you will mail the letters to the teens. These letters, written by their own hands, will serve as powerful reminders to keep them going in the promises they made to the Lord during the Culture Shock event.

After the letters have been collected, we encourage you to close this time by praying over each student and asking God to bless them. If parents are in attendance, have them lead the prayer over their teenagers individually. If the parents are not present, let the teens break up into small groups (five to ten), and assign youth leaders to each group to pray and ask a God-given blessing over each teen. This is a time to bless them and affirm who they are in Christ and encourage them in things like their gifts, call, and destiny.

SUGGESTED PRAYER

We encourage you to personalize these prayers. Here is an example for your leaders to look over:

> *Heavenly Father,*
> *I thank you that _____ is willing to follow after you. Jesus, I ask that you would meet him/her exactly where he/she is, and reveal yourself in a greater way. I thank you that he/she has the amazing gift of _____, and that you will use this gift for your glory. Lord, I ask that he/she would find his/her security and hope in you and you alone. Your Word says, in Zephaniah 3:17, "The LORD your God is with you, the Mighty Warrior who saves. He will take great delight in you; in his love he will no longer rebuke you, but will rejoice over you with singing." I thank you that you rejoice over this life with singing. You take such delight in _____. Lord, I thank you that you will be with _____ all the days of his/her life. In Jesus' name we pray, amen.*

Be sure to include scriptural blessings over each teen. This is critical because the Word of God carries so much power and life when we speak it into lives. Here are some blessing Scriptures we love:

* **Numbers 6:24-26**
* **Deuteronomy 28:6**
* **Psalm 67:1, 2**
* **Proverbs 10:22**
* **Jeremiah 29:11**
* **Ephesians 1:3**
* **Zephaniah 3:17**

YOUR VIEW
Other Scriptures that you feel would fit your particular students:

After you spend time praying over each teen, close with a prayer like the one suggested below, or feel free to offer up your own.

CLOSING PRAYER
God, I thank you that you came to the world to serve humankind. I thank you that you died and rose again. Because of this we have hope for the future. Thank you for the amazing calling and destiny that you have for each and every individual in this place. We ask that you will continue to lead us and guide us as we walk according to the destinies that you have in mind. Help us to better serve others. In Jesus' name we pray, amen.

THE REVOLUTION CONTINUES

First Samuel 16:7 is one of our team's favorite verses. Why? Because it silences every cop-out to fulfilling our God-given calling. Leaders, constantly remind your teens that they have a huge calling in Christ Jesus. More importantly, the extent of their calling does not hinge on appearance, academic achievements, or even the length of their résumés. Look at what God says to the prophet Samuel: "Looks aren't everything. Don't be impressed with his looks and stature. I've already eliminated him. God judges persons differently than humans do. Men and women look at the face; God looks into the heart" (*The Message*).

Here are some sample texts and messages that you can use to encourage your teens:

SAMPLE MESSAGES

- What are your destiny stealers? Check out more in your *Culture Shock* survival guide!

- Go do something completely out of your comfort zone for the kingdom of God. Be sure to share about this experience at youth group. You can do it. (Deut 31:6)

- Can you identify your spiritual gifts? Let the *Culture Shock* survival guide teach you how! (1 Cor 12)

- The key to being a servant is serving. How can you become a better servant at home, at school, and in your community?

- What did the story about King Saul in the survival guide teach you? I want to know!

BUILDING THE BRIDGE

Escaping Normal isn't just an event—it's a life-changing time for many teens. Often, young people have no idea how incredible their purpose and destiny is, and we've found that it is largely a generational issue. It isn't that parents don't believe that their son or daughter *can* do something great; it's just that they don't expect them to. And because no one expects them to, young people rarely are equipped to do anything beyond the status quo—normal.

Every single person on this planet has been placed here for an incredible and awesome reason—that includes every child, every teen, and every parent. So take the time to light a fire not only in the hearts of the teens in your group but also to reach out to the parents and remind them that God is also calling *them* to escape from normal and passionately pursue him. This goes beyond just telling the parents what their kids learned at your event; this is about changing the way families view the callings and purposes of God.

Use the ideas below to connect with parents and to help parents connect with their teens. For more resources, including weekly parent updates and key resource recommendations, visit us online at www.generationsofvirtue.org.

OVERVIEW OF ESCAPING NORMAL

Learning how to serve (servant leadership) is a pivotal step we all need to make when we choose to follow Christ. In this session, we encouraged teens to find ways that they can serve in their everyday lives, ways that they may never receive recognition for.

We highlighted some famous followers of Christ and showcased their humble beginnings. It's truly inspiring to see how faithful God is when we are willing to serve him.

We also focused on the teens' purpose and destiny. We helped them identify what we call destiny stealers—things that take the place of God in our lives, or areas of sin that we can't seem to shake. We believe it's critical to help them see their destiny stealers so that they're able to pray about them, instead of allowing those areas of idolatry or sin to rule.

We ended the event by encouraging teens to dream BIG! We serve an awesome and powerful God, a God who is far from normal! He wants them to do extraordinary things for his kingdom, and he's ready to equip them at every turn, if they'll only look to him as their source and strength.

CONNECT: AN ACTIVITY FOR PARENTS AND TEENS

While it's critical for teens to understand their own destiny stealers, it's also important to identify the things that the enemy would use to steal the destiny of individual families. This week, take time as a family to identify the things that have made their way into your home that should not be there. These could be things such as anger, dishonesty, guilt, negative media influences, and many others.

After you've identified those things together, take time to write out your purpose, vision, and mission as a family. What are your goals to accomplish together? How do you want to treat each other and those around you? What do you want your family's legacy to be? After you've written these things, post them around your home and consider revisiting the concepts every year to see if you need to make any changes or additions.

PLUG IN

Send an e-mail to parents, incorporating the Overview so that they're up to speed on what their teens have experienced and been taught. Continue to keep in touch with them by sending the Connect activity and by using the suggested tweets, Facebook updates, or texts below. Include your contact information so parents can reach you if they have questions.

SAMPLE MESSAGES

- Wow! Your teens have incredible lives ahead of them! Today, ask them what they feel called to do in the future.
- Pray Jeremiah 29:11 over your teen today before school.
- We had an awesome time teaching your kids to identify the destiny stealers in their lives. Ask them what a destiny stealer is! Can you identify yours?
- Encourage your teen in servant leadership today. Point out ways to serve. Set a great example!
- Take a moment and ask your teen today: by the choices you're making, are you blessing your future?
- Do you believe your teen has an extraordinary calling? Say so!

NOTES

1. Drs. Josef Shargorodsky, Sharon G. Curhan, Gary C. Curhan, Roland Eavey, "Change in Prevalence of Hearing Loss in US Adolescents," *JAMA*, August 18, 2010—Vol 304, No. 7, p. 775.

2. Authors' note: This is an activity developed from similar stories of an illustration used to make people think about how they should treat others. The story, sometimes titled "The Dart Test," is often sent as part of an e-mail forward, and as far as we know, the author is unknown.

3. Louann Brizendine, *The Female Brain* (New York: Broadway Books, 2006), 68.

4. Joe McIlhaney and Freda McKissic Bush, *Hooked: New Science on How Casual Sex Is Affecting Our Children* (Northfield Publishing, 2008), 43.

5. www.rand.org/pubs/research_briefs/RB9068/index1.html.

6. "Sexual Lyrics in Popular Songs Linked to Early Sexual Experiences," *Science Daily* (Elsevier Health Sciences), February 25, 2009. Retrieved June 28, 2011, from http://www.sciencedaily.com /releases/2009/02/090224132903.htm.

Facts for the Guess Who activity were gathered from the following sources.
7. 1 Samuel 17; 1 Samuel 16:11; the Psalms.
8. www.heroesofhistory.com/page59.html; www.tlogical.net/bioboom.htm; www.corrietenboom.com /history.htm.
9. www.hyperhistory.net/apwh/bios/b3hudsoneu.htm; www.wholesomewords.org/missions /biotaylor4.html; www.wholesomewords.org/missions/biotaylor2.html; chinese-school.netfirms .com/Christians-in-China.html.
10. Exodus 1:22; Exodus 2:10; Exodus 2:14, 15; Exodus 2 and 3.
11. www.wheaton.edu/bgc/archives/bio.html; www.wheaton.edu/bgc/archives/exhibits/LA49/01intro .html; www.hyperhistory.net/apwh/bios/b4grahambilly.htm.
12. Luke 1:34; Matthew 13:54, 55; Luke 3:23.
13. Brother Andrew, John Sherrill, and Elizabeth Sherrill, *God's Smuggler* (Grand Rapids: Chosen Books, 2001), 74; Janet and Geoff Benge, *Brother Andrew: God's Secret Agent* (Seattle: YWAM Publishing, 2005), 157; www.inspirationalchristians.org/brother-andrew/; www.bookpage.com /9603bp/thecalling/brotherandrew.html.
14. Esther 2:5-9; 7:3, 4.
15. www.hyperhistory.net/apwh/bios/b3carmichaelAmy.html.
16. www.heroesofhistory.com/page46.html; www.tlogical.net/bioaylward.htm.
17. Janet and Geoff Benge, *C. S. Lewis: Master Storyteller* (Seattle: YWAM Publishing, 2007), 38-39; www.cslewis.com/about.aspx.

18. www.goodreads.com/author/quotes/23041.John_Wooden.

ABOUT GENERATIONS OF VIRTUE

The Generations of Virtue team probably isn't what you'd expect. We're just your average globe-trotting, coffee-addicted Jesus freaks who are passionate about spreading God's message of purity and holiness to youth, parents, and pretty much anyone who will listen. When we aren't on the road, we live, work, and play in Colorado Springs, Colorado.

To find out more about us and our mission, programs, resources, and publications, go to www.generationsofvirtue.org.

Pictured (L to R): Katherine Lockhart, Timothy Warner, Julie Hiramine, Courtney Alberson, Kelsey Roberts, Sara Raley, Isaac Roberts, and Megan Briggs.

When is your group doing Culture Shock at your church or event? We want to know! Our team would love to pray for you! Jump onto www.generationsofvirtue .org and let us know!

Encourage your teens to ignite an integrity and purity revolution with *Culture Shock: A Survival Guide for Teens* (ISBN 978-0-7847-3305-9). For more information and to order copies for your group, go to www.standardpub.com or www .generationsofvirtue.org.

GENERATIONS OF VIRTUE

www.generationsofvirtue.org

★ **HUNDREDS** of resources for your group and family

★ Check out our line of **CULTURE SHOCK** rings and apparel

★ **AWESOME** group discounts on purity jewelry

TONS OF FOLLOW UP MATERIALS TO EQUIP YOUR TEENS!

A PURE GENERATION
www.apuregeneration.com